NEW TESTAMENT

General Edito
A.T. Lincoln

ROMANS

ROMANS

Robert Morgan

Sheffield Academic Press

First Published by Sheffield Academic Press 1995
Reprinted 1997

Copyright © 1995, 1997 Sheffield Academic Press

Published by Sheffield Academic Press Ltd
Mansion House
19 Kingfield Road
Sheffield S11 9AS
England

Printed on acid-free paper in Great Britain
by The Cromwell Press
Melksham, Wiltshire

British Library Cataloguing in Publication Data

A catalogue record for this book is available
from the British Library

ISBN 1-85075-739-9

Contents

Acknowledgments

Even a book as small as this one is built upon a pile of debts, more pleasurable than most to recall. Years ago it was a privilege to attend lectures on New Testament theology, mainly on Paul and mainly on Romans, given by Professors C.F.D. Moule, C.K. Barrett and E. Käsemann. Since then these and other teachers have given me generous encouragement to continue, even when I was walking in paths they could hardly approve. Oxford New Testament colleagues, especially John Ashton, Eric Franklin, Chris Rowland, John Muddiman and until recently Ed Sanders have always been willing to share their wisdom and comment on sketches. A succession of students and parishioners have made me want to pass on what I have learned and a patient editor, Andrew Lincoln, provided the stimulus. The opportunity to record these fragments of my gratitude is another reason for writing, as perhaps St Paul thought when dictating ch. 16.

Robert Morgan
St Luke's Day, 1994

1

INTRODUCTION

What's it All About?

ANYONE WHO TRIES TO READ through St Paul's Epistle to the Romans will soon discover it is a dense and difficult text. Modern translations conceal many of the problems by paraphrasing and choosing possible meanings for ambiguous phrases, but the serious student who compares translations or consults a more literal version faces an exegetical minefield. It is wise to be carried through it on the back of a trusted translator, until the text and its background are familiar, and informed decisions between alternative interpretations are possible.

But even modern translations are likely to baffle the average reader, and the reasons lie deeper than Paul's ambiguous phrases. The vocabulary of this text poses two kinds of problem for anyone unfamiliar with its codes. First, words like 'grace' and 'justification' are no longer common coin, and even 'God', 'salvation', and 'faith' are hard to explain in cold blood. Secondly, common words like flesh, law, spirit, and body carry uncommon meanings in Paul's epistles.

That second obstacle can trip up readers who have no problem with the first. These informed readers may also succumb to a third danger: over-familiarity. Some of Paul's words have become commonplace in the Christian doctrinal tradition. But they have a different weight there than here. A knowledge of Christianity can therefore mislead as well as inform our understanding of what this first-century Jewish thinker and activist wrote about God's messiah and the implications of his arrival.

These cautions must be balanced by the simple fact that Romans has over nineteen centuries established itself among learned and unlearned alike as one of the richest writings ever penned. Its impact has been incalculable, and if that stems partly from thoughts that would have surprised Paul himself the same can be said of much great literature.

That raises a number of issues to be addressed before turning to the text itself. A 'New Testament Guide' should say at the outset what kind of guidance it will provide.

The aim of this book is to help readers understand St Paul's Epistle to the Romans. It is not a book about the Greek language, ancient letter-writing, or rhetoric. Those specialist studies contribute to understanding this highly rhetorical Hellenistic Greek letter, but their focus is different. The questions they ask are not those the text or author intended to answer.

It is also slightly different from books which use Romans to reconstruct the early history of Christianity or to sketch the apostle's theology, or to inform and structure a modern Christian's faith. These larger enterprises draw data from the epistle and may also throw light on it. Letters are not written in a vacuum and theological compositions like this one express their author's whole view of Christianity. The relationship between Romans and subsequent Christianity is also worth exploring (see ch. 6). But our aim here is firstly more narrowly focused. The text has an integrity of its own, regardless of our reasons for studying it, whether these are historical or theological. We want to respect that and understand the epistle in its own terms without rushing to claim it for our own religious or academic projects. How deeply a religious text can be understood in abstraction from religious practice is a moot point, but some measure of understanding must be possible, otherwise there would be no communication between insiders and outsiders.

In treating this part of Christian Scripture as a piece of (religious) literature the first step must be to classify it, that is, determine its *genre*, or what *kind* of a text it is. Plainly it was written and received as a *letter*, and letters—even official letters—are more rooted in a particular context than most literature. Historical questions are important here because Romans was written to and from a specific situation before it was Christian Scripture. It has not ceased to be a letter even though the original recipients and the author are long dead and it has been given a new context and new functions. We want to know what writers of letters were wanting to say and are uneasy about importing meanings which the author could never have intended.

There are other reasons for respecting the author's intentions in this case, in contrast to poems and psalms that are less tied to their creators. Romans has proved central for defining Western Christianity. Theories about human nature and destiny, about the church, Israel, the state, even the created order, have hinged on how this epistle is read. With so much at stake, and such scope for disagreement, those whose thoughts and lives are fired by this epistle need a criterion for sorting out the disputes that have in the past proved divisive. Even if Paul's own intentions are hard to determine with any certainty, the effort will inject some controls into the ongoing conversation with and about this classic text.

A historical approach to this writing offers one way of beginning to discover what it is all about. We know a lot about the author and his situation and that should throw light on his epistle. Anyone who thinks Paul has something of value to say, and who wants to hear it, will take historical research seriously. But the light it gives is partial, and no one who is stirred by the question of God can stop there when studying a religious text. Limiting our focus to the text before us is less ambitious than some larger historical projects, but what is envisaged here is also more ambitious than a historical scholarship which does not try to explain what the text is all about. Our aim to understand the epistle will lead us, however tentatively, in the direction of theological interpretation. Taking this ancient text as it stands requires in addition to the basic linguistic, historical and literary skills, a frame of reference to understand what Paul was getting at. The epistle purports to speak of things which eye has not seen, 'the depth of the riches and wisdom and

knowledge of God' whose 'judgments are unsearchable, his
ways inscrutable' (11.33). How are we to make sense of that?
Some will see no problem here. Clearly Romans is about
God and Christ and humanity and salvation. Whether or not
Paul is right about these matters is a further question which
would involve discussing the truth of Christianity, but his
subject-matter itself is not in dispute. However, God and the
gospel of salvation are more elusive than that common-sense
approach admits. It is not just that some say God exists and
salvation is a reality, whereas others deny it, but that the
meaning of these terms is disputed. Those who use the words
in religious contexts are doing something different and might
mean something different from those who consider them
vacuous. It seems that how we understand these words of
Paul depends partly on how or what we think about the
reality to which they claim to refer. Simply repeating the
Christian words reduces them to ciphers and cannot be
called understanding Paul's epistle as he intended to be
understood.

To say Romans is about God and salvation is at best a
shorthand, because talk of God itself needs decoding. Some
Christians very familiar with Paul's religious language may
not see a problem because they are silently assimilating it
into their own religious life and experience. Their whole view
of themselves and the world has been so shaped by Paul's
language that they feel at home with it. For many today,
however, it is an unfamiliar language, foreign to their experience and understanding of themselves and the world. But
other people's systems deserve respect, and the greatest
respect one can pay a text is to try and understand it. Our
question is, how can outsiders crack the code?

The simple answer, since Romans is clearly a religious
text, is to say that it is about religion, a well-known human
phenomenon that has been observed and analysed as well as
practised. This does not sidestep all the difficulties inherent
in God language because how we think of religion may also
be affected by our own religious beliefs or lack of them. But
competing accounts of religion can be assessed by reference
to empirical data, whereas beliefs in God and salvation are
harder to evaluate.

There is not space here to develop a comprehensive theory of religion and defend it against other theories (e.g. Marxist and Freudian) which deny the reality of God; nor to distinguish it from theories of revelation which presuppose the truth of Christianity. To allow believers and non-believers to discuss the religious subject-matter of Romans, such a comprehensive theory of religion would have to be open to the possibility that Paul was mostly right (as Christians by and large assume) without actually making that claim. Social anthropologists can describe religions as 'systems of symbols' comprising rituals, beliefs, and moral patterns, expressing human meanings and values and motivations by reference to a transcendent. Whether or not living within a system of religious practice and belief actually puts people in touch with ultimate reality (if such a phrase is meaningful) is an open question, but analysing religions in this way provides a frame of reference for understanding or making sense of a religious text.

That might seem pointless to believers whose understanding of Romans is guided and deepened by their own Christian frameworks of belief and practice. But as well as providing a language through which everyone can see and say what Romans is about, the change of perspective may prove suggestive for believers. Reading this weighty epistle without the customary spectacles of a Christian doctrinal framework may avoid some distortions arising from later tradition and experience.

Holding theological convictions in suspense while trying to make sense of Romans has enabled Christian commentators since Grotius in the mid-seventeenth century to see the text afresh, to correct older interpretations and make new proposals. That has been the main value of historical exegesis to Christian theology. It has advanced reflection on these classic texts and so stimulated reflection and criticism of contemporary belief and practice. But unless it is broadened out by perspectives drawn from the historical and social scientific study of religion in general, that purely historical study of the New Testament can easily lose sight of its subject matter. The historian's legitimate interest in why Paul wrote and where he derived his ideas from then becomes a substitute for describing the elusive subject-matter of this text. Christian doctrinal language identifies and interprets realities of faith and so helps some readers take what Paul says as seriously as he intended. But in a secular society that does not work for everyone. Language used by anthropologists in analysing religion provides an alternative vocabulary for understanding what Paul wrote.

This proposal for interpreting Romans theologically does not require reconstructing Paul's own religion in historical detail. Neither does it mean imposing a theory of religion upon the text. Our aim is simply to understand Romans as the religious text it is, instead of reducing it to some other form of communication. That will provide a corrective to recent emphases on purely historical questions. These are necessary aids to understanding what Paul wanted his hearers and readers to understand, and historians are free to restrict themselves in this way, but those who wish to under-stand what Paul wrote in accord with his own intentions will have to approach him with some language for talking about religion. Christian theology provides this, but those who do not read Romans from within a Christian context need a language that makes fewer assumptions. Modern analyses of religions provide terms which Christians assume may refer to a relationship to God, but this assumption is not required of anyone analysing a religion or understanding a religious text in these terms.

All this is to say that there is more to understanding Romans than translating Greek into English or selecting the most likely meaning of Paul's many ambiguous phrases. Different kinds of texts require different competences and this one requires some understanding of religion as well as historical and literary skills. Most students have some idea about religion before they read Romans, and no more is needed than that which would find wide agreement.

Our starting-point, then, is a desire to understand what Paul intended his audience to understand, and a recognition that this was to do with what we call religion, his own reli-gion and theirs. Exegetical disagreements will emerge, requiring the scholarly conversation about this text to continue alongside its religious apprehension. How they are resolved will often depend on the interpreter's sense of the whole structure and direction of its argument, the author's purposes in writing and the persons and circumstances addressed. These all call for hypotheses which may be confirmed or corrected by subsequent readings. The reader's constant to and fro between the whole text and its parts should uncover the shape of the argument or exposition, and show how the various sections are related. That will be reinforced by a further to and fro between the literary text and the history which apparently evoked it. A hypothetical reconstruction of the historical context, like each exegetical decision, will satisfy if it illuminates the larger whole and allows this to make an impact on the reader.

We do not possess the letter exactly as it left Paul (and Tertius, 16.22). There is always the possibility of minor glosses and interpolations as well as copyists' errors. But there is no reason to doubt that our critically reconstructed Greek texts are broadly accurate. Interpolation hypotheses are so speculative that they need only be discussed when the arguments for them seem very strong. We can start with what we have in our printed English translations. Sixteen centuries ago Romans entered the soul of Western Christianity and culture when a voice told Augustine to 'pick up and read' (Confessions 9). It did not tell him to read the Greek, nor did it tell him which translation to use. His Greek was weak and Jerome's new Latin Bible, the Vulgate, had not yet reached Romans. We can begin where we are, with whatever translation we possess, and save till later the fascination of comparing two or more translations. Meanwhile, where your translation differs from phrases discussed below, it is safe to assume that Paul's Greek is ambiguous.

2

A FIRST ATTEMPT
AT READING

UNDERSTANDING A DENSE and difficult text is largely a process of reading and re-reading, sometimes with the help of some background information. We shall start slowly and accelerate as the text begins to make sense. There is not the space in this Guide to go through the whole epistle a second and a third time. Some details more appropriately left till later must therefore be included here. Most students may be advised to skim this chapter or use it selectively at their first reading (with the text of Romans alongside), and return to it again and again—still with the text of Romans in their hand or head—after reading (in any order) bits of the following chapters of this Guide. A first attempt at reading Romans may not get very much further than grasping the shape and general content of the whole. Following an introduction its major structural divisions fall after chs. 4 (or 5?), 8, 11, and 15. Those four main sections are largely about (1) God's righteousness being from faith (not works of the law); (2) Christian existence and experience—freedom from sin and law, life in the Spirit; (3) Israel's unbelief and salvation; and (4) moral admonitions. The final chapter contains lengthy greetings.

That description of the first section does not say anything about the most difficult and contested part of the epistle, 1.18–3.18. Neither does it explain what is meant by 'God's righteousness'. The conflict of interpretations is fiercest in these first chapters, and Paul's text mocks our Guide's attempt to 'keep it simple'. Not every exegetical and interpretative possibility can be noted in a student's early readings. Keeping it short will allow us to see the wood through the trees.

1.1-15
Like the original recipients in Rome, most readers know before they start who Paul is. He introduces himself in a long opening sentence as 'a servant (or slave) of Christ Jesus, called (to be an) apostle, set apart for (the task of communicating the) gospel of God, which God promised beforehand through his prophets in holy scriptures concerning his Son...'

Several striking ideas are introduced here without explanation. Paul can assume they understand his insider language. They know who Christ (Messiah) Jesus is, and what an apostle is, what the Scriptures are, and that God is an agent who has made promises through the prophets. These prophets are said to refer to a person who is called God's Son, and Paul himself has a God-given role to spread a message about him which is described (without explanation) as gospel of God. That might mean from God, or concerning God, or belonging to God—or all of these. Paul's 'ofs' are often ambiguous, but it is not always necessary to choose one meaning and exclude the rest.

God's Son is then described and identified in a couplet which contains ideas and phrases not found elsewhere in Paul's writings, and so looks like a quotation from some early Christian creed or confession used in worship. Jesus is descended from David as regards his human origin, and appointed or designated Son of God (cf. 2 Sam. 7.14) in power 'according to a spirit of holiness resulting from a resurrection of dead people'. Both the Spirit (cf. Acts 2.17) and a resurrection of dead people (cf. Dan. 12.2) were associated by many Jews with the expected end of the 'present evil age' (cf. Gal. 1.4). Apparently like the first followers (cf. 1 Cor. 15.11), Paul saw Jesus' resurrection as the dawn of the age to come and the beginning of a more general resurrection to new life (cf. 1 Cor. 15.20; Rom. 8.29).

Three times in this long opening sentence Jesus is called

messiah, another 'end time' or eschatological word. That
most frequent New Testament title for Jesus has already
become a name by v. 4. It is combined in vv. 4 and 7, as often
in this epistle and elsewhere (e.g. Acts 2.36) with the title
Lord, which Paul uses about 200 times; this second title
corresponds to the self-designation in v. 1: slave. It seems
that Paul thought of himself as a servant of the Lord like the
prophet in Isa. 49.1-6.

He then (v. 5) insists that his own apostleship came
through this risen Lord as a gift and task to bring about
obedience of faith (another ambiguous and so pregnant genitive or 'of' phrase) among all nations or Gentiles. That all (v.
5) includes all (v. 7) those he is now addressing in Rome (a
few manuscripts omit 'in Rome' here and in v. 14). They too
are called by and belong to Jesus Christ. They are beloved of
God, called (repeated a third time), saints. The word
'Christians' introduced at Acts 11.26 (cf. 26.28; 1 Pet. 4.16) is
not found in Paul's epistles.

Paul's usual Christian greeting follows the standard
pattern for Greek letter-openings (From A, to B, greetings),
and boosts it with theological content. He then starts in all
his epistles except Galatians with a thanksgiving. He thanks
God through Jesus Christ, again for *all* of them, and the
repetition may be significant. Their faith is spoken of world-
wide and Paul assures them of his unceasing prayers for
them. That includes his hopes of visiting them and sharing
his gift, and strengthening them—or rather (he adds tactfully) that he and they should be encouraged by each other's
faith. He has to communicate the gospel to *all* Gentiles, and
that includes those in Rome.

1.16-17
Paul now specifies 'the gospel' as he understands and
confesses it: a power of God (leading) to salvation for
everyone who believes, Jew first and Greek, that is, Gentile.
Another all. He elaborates this, echoing one of the key
concepts just introduced (believing) and introducing another
pair of related (*dik-*) words which will dominate this epistle.
These have a forensic (law-courts) background, and often a
moral flavour. Both aspects imply right relationships, but are
hard to translate well because no translation will convey the

weight they are going to bear in what follows and even the translation of *pistis* as faith is now contested; faithfulness is an alternative possibility. But to start with a conventional translation: 'In it (the gospel) *righteousness* of God is being revealed from *faith* to *faith*, as it is written the *righteous* from faith person shall live' (or: the righteous one shall live from faith). Whatever this means, it looks like a statement of Paul's theme in Romans. He is going to communicate his own understanding of the Christian message which vv. 3-4 summarized in the credal terms probably already familiar to them. That message 'concerning his Son' stems from and is empowered by God, and is directed towards humans' ultimate well-being or salvation. Who God *is* can be taken as read, known from holy Scriptures and through the Jewish religious tradition in which Paul and his hearers stand. The prophets point forward to the life (v. 17) which Paul now proclaims is for *all* who believe, Jew first and Gentile.

The subject of his message was evidently well-known, but the key terms in which (for reasons not yet clear) he will explain it are partly new. They are adumbrated in the quotation from Hab. 2.4.

Faith or faithfulness (the noun) and having faith (the verb) are very common words in Paul's writings and throughout the early Christian mission. The noun has already occurred three times (vv. 5, 8 and 12) before these three further occurrences in v. 17. The verb 'to have faith', trust, or believe, also occurs in v. 16. Righteous, righteousness, and (later) the verb 'to put right' or 'make righteous' are far less common in Paul and other Christian writers, but very familiar to them from their Greek Bible, the Septuagint (LXX). In this epistle they will be as important as faith or faithfulness and believing. The phrase 'righteousness of God' in v. 17 is programmatic and will recur at 3.5, 21, 22 (25, 26); 10.3. Apart from an obscure verse, 2 Cor. 5.21, it is not found in Paul's writings outside Romans, not even in Galatians which in some other and related respects is very similar to Romans.

What exactly Paul's phrase 'righteousness of God' means has been much debated since Augustine made it central for the theology of the Middle Ages, leading to its impact on the young Augustinian monk Martin Luther (see ch. 6). They all used the word *iustitia*, justice, still preferred in some English translations, which suggests the stern philosophical meaning of 'giving to everyone their just deserts' rather than the passionate religious connotations it often has in the Greek Psalter and Isaiah. Luther found his understanding of Christianity revolutionized by taking the ambiguous 'of' as 'righteousness *from* God' (cf. Phil. 3.9), that is, a *gift from* God rather than a *quality of* God (his character). He had been taught that it meant God was just and would therefore punish sinners, but then he noticed that Paul's context implies a positive sense referring to salvation, and so interpreted the phrase in connection with faith, as the salvation that God gives.

But why does Paul use this judicial metaphor suggesting vindication in a law court?

We can see from his quotations that the origins of Paul's 'right' language are biblical. Gen. 15.6 (which contains the noun) is quoted in Galatians 3 and Romans 4; Hab. 2.4 (which contains the adjective) at Gal. 3.11 and Rom. 1.17; and Ps. 143.2 (which contains the verb) is echoed at Gal. 2.16 and Rom. 3.20. It is natural to suppose that the Romans phrase 'God's righteousness' also derives from that source. Parallels in Qumran and other post-biblical Jewish literature are important, but less so than the main source of Paul's religious discourse, his Scriptures. One reason why he used them was to prove a point, since Scripture was authoritative for both Paul and his hearers. More importantly, religious talk of God generally draws on the speaker's already existing tradition, and in many religions Scripture is the basic tradition and resource.

Fourteen of the fifty-odd quotations from the Septuagint in Romans are from the Psalter, which is second only to Isaiah. Out of some eighty references to God's righteousness in the Psalter, over half are at least loosely concerned with salvation. It is plausible to see in Rom. 1.16-17 an echo of Ps. 97.2 in the LXX (Hebrew and English 98.2): 'The Lord made known his salvation (*soterion*; Rom. 1.16 has *soterian*). In the presence of the Gentiles (God) revealed his righteousness' (aorist active; Paul's divine passive 'is being revealed', i.e. by God, has the present tense of the same verb). The Psalm says 'his', meaning God's righteousness. What God is now doing among the Gentiles is a main theme of Paul's letter and may explain his recourse to the Psalter's references to the nations and to God's 'righteousness' and 'salvation' being declared to them. What exactly this means for them is not explained, but like most of Scripture it refers to human life in this world and includes right relationships of justice and peace under God's care and guidance. Paul looks forward to future transformation, but draws on this-worldly biblical eschatology to describe the new age he sees dawning in the death and resurrection of Christ This saving revelation of God's faithfulness (3.3) is now available to Jews and Gentiles alike.

Neither the Psalter nor Deutero-Isaiah, which together provide most of the theological and moral vocabulary of Romans, connect God's or human righteousness with faith. That connection is Paul's main interest and he had already found it in Gen. 15.6 and Hab. 2.4 when he wrote Galatians. The association of being 'right' with God and 'faith' *in*, and possibly the faithfulness *of* Christ is central to both epistles and to Philippians 3. It has in recent years been explained on the historical plane of Paul's own Gentile mission (see below, chs. 3 and 4), and for centuries on the theological plane of what Paul at Gal. 2.5, 14 calls 'the truth of the gospel'. Both types of explanation are correct, but the details are open to debate.

Our suggestion that Paul draws on the Psalms which speak of God's righteousness or salvation or glory being declared or revealed or gospelled among all nations or peoples or Gentiles, will find support in our later discussions of the historical context of the epistle, and our examination of Paul's biblical quotations (e.g. Rom. 15.9-12). But already the attempt to read through the epistle has run into problems. Key words and phrases have already occurred and called for detailed explanation, and there is room for disagreement. Second Isaiah is widely admitted to contain a key to Paul's use of the verb 'to put right, vindicate or justify', but the Psalter has not usually been proposed as the main source of his phrase 'God's righteousness'—perhaps because the precise formulation does not occur there—even though the

noun and the sense of the phrase are common. Our suggestion needs elaboration and must await confirmation (or
disconfirmation) from the sense it makes of the whole epistle.
Paul's introduction of his theme at 1.16-17 has opened a
wide door for debate and any conclusions about what he
means here must depend on what follows. But that too has
been understood in different ways. Tracing Paul's argument
opens up so many possibilities that we need a historical
hypothesis about his aims to guide us through the maze of
exegetical alternatives. This must itself be based on a preliminary assessment of what he seems to be emphasizing and
anything we can discover about his circumstances in writing.
Not even that will enable us fully to decode Paul's strange
language and catch all its nuances. Readers may also draw
on their own understanding of religion or experience of
Christianity to help them to make sense of this text. But if
Paul's aims and context can be reconstructed that will
provide some control against the subjectivity involved in any
attempt to understand what an apostle says about God.

Paul's emphasis on 'all' in vv. 5, 7, 8 and 16, neglected in
accounts of v. 16 which discuss only God and salvation, will
be illuminated by what follows, and in the next chapter of
this Guide. Paul's actual concerns in his Gentile mission help
explain what he wrote. The first step, however, is to become
sufficiently familiar with the text itself to frame a reasonable
hypothesis. That involves seeing its structure and shape, and
the outline of its argument or exposition. The full meaning of
his language and why he chose it, and the resolution of some
exegetical ambiguities, must wait upon further soundings.

1.18–3.20
After introducing his key terms in v. 17 ('right' language, and
'faith' or believing) by saying what is already happening in
the 'power of God leading to salvation' which he calls 'the
gospel', Paul seems to digress before returning to his theme
in more detail at 3.21. Those thematic statements about the
righteousness of God in 1.17 and 3.21 place a bracket around
1.18–3.20 and imply that this is a single section of the
epistle, though 3.19-20 sits uncomfortably on the end—which
may be revealing—and points forward to what follows.

What Paul is saying and why he is saying it have been much disputed recently. Rom. 1.18-32 describes the vices of the Gentile world in the standard terms of Jewish apologetic and polemic. It claims that God is letting them stew in their own vice. Echoing stoic natural theology, Paul argues that all humanity has some knowledge of God and is therefore morally accountable (vv. 19-20). Chapter 2 is more difficult, as it is not clear who is being accused in vv. 1-16. Whoever it is, they are said to be guilty too. From v. 17 to the end of the chapter some Jews are addressed and accused, and they could be in mind in the earlier part of the chapter, though the conversation-partner in this imaginary dialogue is more likely to be a Gentile, because the 'wherefore' links the passage to 1.18-32.

1.18 begins with a statement that God's wrath is being revealed. Paul is not embarrassed by Scripture's anthropomorphism. God is personal and hates human wickedness. The verbal parallel with God's righteousness being revealed (1.17) and the eschatological connotations of 'wrath' (cf. 2.5, 8) have led many to see here God's final judgment as already operative, working itself out in history. But Paul goes on to speak in traditional Jewish terms (2.5-10) of the *future* eschatological judgment according to works. 1.18-32 is different. It is linked to what precedes by an explanatory 'for' and clarifies the situation in which the gospel of salvation is now being proclaimed. It is not itself part of the gospel. The world is in a mess and God is already angry with human moral failure. God's 'wrath' is no more eschatological at 1.18 than in Ps. 95(LXX 94).11. The passage perhaps echoes missionary preaching to Gentiles (cf. 1. Thess. 1.9-10). While addressing Gentile believers (1.5, 11.13), as at least part of his audience, Paul could also be reassuring Jewish-Christian hearers that controversial though his Gentile mission was, he still shares the usual Jewish criticisms of Gentile vice.

It is harder to see what he is getting at in ch. 2. A representative Jewish teacher is criticized in vv. 17-24 and a conclusion about circumcision is drawn in vv. 25-29. The link with ch. 1 and the conclusion that are all under sin (3.9) have led most commentators to assume that the whole chapter is intended to support this conclusion by finding all Jews (or

Judaism as a whole) guilty of the failures attacked in vv. 17-24. Paul might have argued that weakly, but it is very unlikely that he thought the Jewish world as reprobate as the Gentile. They had significant advantages (3.2), whatever the obscure verse 3.9 means, and despite the rhetorical exaggerations of the string of texts in 3.10-18 which perhaps already existed as a lament. Paul did not need to prove that all are under sin, and his insistence that Jews are included may have a different motive. The way it is picked up by the *all* in 3.23, and the way that 'all' corresponds to the 'all who have faith' in 3.22 suggests that Paul is here insisting that all share the same plight because he wants to insist that all are put right in the same way, not because he has to argue that all need to be put right. Nobody was denying that. The question was how, and Paul's answer was in all cases, Jew and Gentile, by faith. His appeal to the undisputed axiom of God's impartiality at 2.11 is not primarily theodicy, as some suggest. It reinforces the point that God treats Jews and Gentiles in the same way, as a just judge and a saviour (cf. Isa. 45.21), and so helps Paul make the transition from his moral condemnation and warning, to his theological thesis about everyone being put right on a basis of faith.

Elsewhere Paul cannot accept that Jewish privileges (the law) render God's saving righteousness, which is now revealed in Christ, unnecessary (Gal. 2.21). That must surely be his conviction here too, contrary to some interpretations of ch. 11. But for reasons not yet clarified he is at this point edging quite cautiously in this direction, moving from a statement about the law that no Jew would deny (2.13), to a more debatable relativizing of physical circumcision (2.25-29). He is quietly making room for his thesis about Gentile inclusion, and its implication that they do not require circumcision. His note on divine impartiality links the demand for moral responsibility, reinforced by the positive note about some Gentiles at 2.14-15, with his main missionary concern (1.5) for the inclusion of Gentiles as *Gentiles* (cf. Gal. 2.14) on a basis which gives them equal access to the grace (3.24; 6.14) of God.

The mainly moral, apologetic, and missionary focus of Paul's concern in chs. 1–2, and the absence of any reference to eschatological judgment in ch. 1, make us question the usual forensic interpretations of the phrase 'righteousness of God' (1.17; 3.21-26; 10.3). Luther broke with the dominant medieval image of the divine judge punishing sinners but retained the legal frame of reference. It survived in Protestantism, even when qualified by the modern rediscovery of eschatology. Thus Bultmann's 'forensic eschatological' interpretation suggests that Paul is thinking of the Great Assize, but sees its positive verdict on believers anticipated already in their present.

But making the Last Judgment the key to Paul's language obscures the joyful celebration of God's righteousness in Romans and the Psalter, and reinterpreting that expectation existentially to refer to the present is scarcely compatible with the traditional future language about it used at 2.5-10. Like Matthew and the Book of Revelation, Paul can talk of future salvation in apocalyptic terms, and sees the new age operative in the Spirit, but probably does not mean by 'righteousness' future salvation, already imputed to believers in the present.

What God is doing now in the gospel (1.17) is 'eschatological' in the sense of being connected with Jewish expectations of the coming of Messiah and the end of the present evil age. Believers are rescued from that (Gal. 1.4) and experience in the gift of the Spirit the first instalment of the age to come (2 Cor. 1.22; cf. Rom. 8.23). The generally forensic background of 'right' language must also be conceded, and the verb at 2.13 can be labelled 'forensic eschatological'—though that is so untypical that it cannot be made a key to Paul's usage. The righting verb is also forensic in the Psalm quotations at 3.4 (LXX Ps. 50.6) and 3.20 (LXX Ps. 142.2). The scriptural metaphor draws this part of Paul's language in a forensic direction. But instead of aligning it with his prior beliefs about a future judgment, and finding judgment and salvation already present in a person's response to Christ (as Jn 3.17-21 does), Paul draws on other aspects of Isaiah and the Psalter's 'right' language: these speak of God's decisive intervention in this world, and the good of it all. The forensic metaphor has in most passages lost its stern aspect of judgment.

The probable background to 1.17 (cf. 3.21-26; 10.3) in Ps. 96 (LXX 95).10, 13 and Ps. 98 (LXX 97).11 may be called forensic in that the Psalmist looks forward to God vindicating his people and establishing justice on earth. Paul sets this in the eschatological context of the coming of Messiah. But what he is celebrating is the dawn of future salvation, not its proleptic realization—God's new move on behalf of Gentiles, not the anticipation of the Last Judgment, as though its rewards and punishments were already a reality. Paul's understanding of Christian existence remains brutally this-worldly. His hope of resurrection life in the age to come does not deprive his present earthly life and activity of their significance. The power of the Spirit, active in Paul's own gift or grace (see below p. 122), energizes him to fulfil his missionary task in this temporal world.

It is important to relate Paul's 'right' language to salvation rather than to the punishment due to sinners. The theme of divine retribution is introduced briefly at 1.32 and 2.5-16 to insist that all are accountable, not (as in Mt. 25 and Rev. 20) to draw Paul's righteousness language into relationship with the Great Assize. But it is also important to distinguish between what God is doing now to make salvation possible for all, Jews and Gentiles alike, and the future realization of salvation itself. As he articulates his gospel in 'right' terms in Romans, Galatians, and Philippians 3, but not much elsewhere, their intention and meaning must be related to his purposes in these epistles, not abstracted from the missionary situation and treated as parts of a general doctrinal system. Even if they should prove the most illuminating of all Paul's metaphors, and the most universally applicable, they must first be interpreted in historical context.

That is far from clear in Romans and one task of a first reading is to notice features of the text which might be relevant to framing a hypothesis about it. For example, the usual view that in 1.18–3.20 Paul is underlining that all need salvation can be co-ordinated with a possible intention by Paul to provide a systematic exposition of his thought. But while fitting 1.18-32, this reading makes the whole section into an implausible argument. The alternative emphasis on

all, Jews and Gentiles, being in the same situation fits better
with what Paul will say at 3.21-22 about all being put right
in the same way, and fits an alternative explanation of Paul's
aims and the situation to which he was writing.

Again, a striking feature of ch. 2 might reveal something of
Paul's purpose. In Romans as in Galatians Paul has much to
say about the Jewish law, some of it negative. But none of
the 18 instances of the word in 2.12-27 is negative, and the
law was not mentioned in his thematic statement at 1.16-17.
The negative statement (not by works) appears rather
abruptly at the end of the blanket condemnation in this
section 1.18–3.20. It then recurs forcefully in 3.21ff., as the
negative side of an antithesis: salvation (righteousness of
God) is not that way (from works of law) but this way (by or
through or from faith). Chapter 2 is odd in how much it
speaks of law or the law without yet introducing this fundamental antithesis of faith and works. Verses 12-16 and even
17-24 are quite positive about the Jewish law. Only vv. 25-29
begin to relativize it. Paul is treading so carefully that it is
hard to doubt that what he has to say about the law lies at
the heart of this epistle. It keeps cropping up, without being
handled directly and thematically as yet.

What Paul says here about law and circumcision may turn
out to be related to all that follows, but as yet only the sinful-
ness and accountability of both Jews and Gentiles without
difference is registered. It is not even clear what Gentiles
Paul has in mind—Gentiles in general or Gentile Christians.

It is, however, clear from 3.1-3 that Paul's argument can
already be construed as depriving the Jewish people of their
special status as God's people. This throws into question
God's reliability and faithfulness to the promises made in the
past (v. 3). Paul's convictions about what God is now doing
for Gentiles demand an interpretation of God's promises and
an explanation justifying God's treatment of Israel. This will
follow in chs. 9–11, but a marker is laid at this point.

Paul's not requiring observance of Torah from his Gentile
converts also raises questions about morality. In fact questions have been raised (3.8) about the moral implications of
Paul's understanding of the gospel. The heavy moralizing of
ch. 1 may have been composed with that in mind. Paul is not

soft on morality—he insists on God's judgment as strongly as anyone. And yet, when he picks up the language of the Psalter and talks of God's righteousness and humans' true righteousness, it is to articulate good news from God. The note of judgment is inescapable when speaking of the God of Israel who is a God of justice and truth, but God's rule and righteousness are proclaimed as good news of salvation among the nations in Psalms 96–98. For Paul, too, the revelation of God's righteousness is good news, and his use of the Septuagint verb 'to make right', which translates the Hebrew for vindication in a law court, echoes this. God's present anger against wickedness is real, and future judgment inescapable, but the righteousness of God, operative in the sending of the Son (8.3) and his sacrificial death and the formation of a new world through his resurrection from the dead, heralds salvation. Paul's noun has scarcely a trace of the law court, or of justice requiring punishment or satisfaction, contrary to a common misreading of 3.25 as an explanation of the Atonement.

The problems raised in 3.1-8 are not yet resolved and will be taken up later in the epistle. But they seem so important that we may already suspect they are central to Paul's purposes in writing. Paul rebuts one objection with a scriptural flourish, the other with a dismissive wave. Neither is an answer, though both show what Paul takes for granted about God. The root of both issues—the alleged loss of Israel's privileges and the threat to morality—can only be what Paul has to say about the Jewish law. Chapter 2 disallowed its role as a boundary between Jews and Gentiles. Morality is obligatory but circumcision (that marker of male Jewish identity) is really an inner matter of the spirit, not an outer matter in the flesh. That goes a step further than the remark in v. 13 (which no Jew would dispute) that it is not hearing the law that makes you right with God, but doers of it who will be righted, vindicated, acquitted, justified, rectified, rightwised—or however one chooses to translate the 'righting' verb. E.P. Sanders's coinage 'to righteous' highlights the problem, but 'righteous' in English is ethical; Paul's religious meaning 'to put in a right relationship (with God)' (2.13; 5.19) places the accents elsewhere.

Everyone is accountable, or liable to judgment (3.19b); that has been said from 1.18 on. But the two transitional verses 3.19-20 are far from clear. It may be that when Paul begins to talk about the Jewish law more directly he is pulled in different directions.

The addition of 'from works of law' to the echo of Ps. 143 (LXX 142).2 in v. 20.(as also in Gal. 2.16) looks at first sight as though Paul is slipping into scripture the conclusion he wants to draw out from it. But this interpretative addition is defensible if one thinks the Psalmist (and Jews who prayed through the Psalter) come to the seat of judgment from lives lived doing what the law requires. When they denied anyone could earn acquittal, and prayed that God would hear them in God's faithfulness and righteousness (LXX Ps. 142.1) they could be thought to be saying that there was no 'being righted' to be found from within their system of law.

Paul will take up his last remark in 3.20, that through law comes awareness of sin, in ch .7. It seems that in addition to drawing the conclusion from 1.18–2.24 that all, Jews and Gentiles, are under sin, ch. 3 lays down a number of markers for future discussion. Verses 1-3 are taken up in chs. 9–11; vv. 7-8 in ch. 6; v. 20a here; v. 20b in chs. 5 and 7; and v. 31 in chs. 4, 7, 8, 10, 13. These points are all concerned with the law, the first two indirectly, the last three directly, and that suggests that the law is somehow Paul's main concern in this epistle, even though it is not his explicit theme.

The central issue among the five markers (20a: not by works) is taken up at once. 3.21-30 echoes the thematic statement of 1.17, but amplifies it in several ways, above all by creating an antithesis: (the way to salvation) is *this* way—by faith, *not* that way—by Torah observance. 1.16 had already insisted this applies to every believer, Jew first and Greek. 3.22 repeats that point, relating it to the discussion in ch. 2.

3.21-31

3.21 begins the new sub-section with a strong contrast to what has gone before. Its importance and centrality are plain as it picks up the thematic statement of 1.17, expands it, and debates its consequences (vv. 27-31), before confirming it in ch. 4 by argument from Scripture. Paul varies his verb and

tense from the present 'is being revealed' in 1.17 to the
perfect (= completed action in the past) 'has been made
manifest' at 3.21, presumably because he is about to discuss
the past death of Jesus, whereas in 1.17 he was speaking of
the present operation of the gospel. God's right or saving
action (cf. Isa. 45.21) has both a past and a present aspect, as
well as a future consummation. It is being revealed now in
present Christian proclamation actualizing the past event of
Jesus' death and resurrection.

In vv. 21-22 the positive statement about God's righteousness having been made plain, and being received by the
human response of faith, is expanded by an exclusion of law.
This develops the negation introduced at v. 20a into an
informal antithesis. It is similar to Gal. 2.16–3.12 and Phil.
3.9, but here in Romans the antithesis is immediately
qualified by Paul giving some positive significance to the
Jewish law. As part of Scripture it bears witness to this
'righteousness of God' (v. 21b). The peculiar phrase 'law of
faith' (contrasted with 'law of works' in v. 27) must also have
a positive meaning, and at the end of these vital few verses
Paul claims not to be annulling but to be establishing the law
(v. 31). That comes as a surprise, because the main point of
vv. 21-30 is that the righteousness of God is 'through faith of
Jesus Christ towards all who believe' (v. 22), apart from law
(v. 21) or works of law (v. 28). But Paul presumably means
what he says, and exegesis must explain this qualification of
the negative statements about the law in 3.20-30. Paul
qualifies his denial of the law's place in the present revelation of God's righteousness with an affirmation of its positive
role, at least as witness, and apparently in other functions
(3.20b).

A second major addition to 1.17 in this new thematic statement is its references to Jesus and his death, here understood as a sacrifice. In Paul's letters faith and believing
usually seem to relate people (i.e. Christians) to Christ, and
so to refer to Christian faith. Rom. 3.3 is an exception, referring to the faithfulness of God, and the phrases 'faith (or
faithfulness) of Jesus Christ' in v. 22 and 'of Jesus' in v. 26
are peculiar. They are naturally taken to refer to Jesus' own
faith or faithfulness, and some read them that way. The

majority who take Paul to mean faith *in* Jesus (i.e. in God through Jesus as at Gal. 2.16b) have to explain Paul's odd genitive ('of') here and in Gal. 2.16a and c, 20; 3.22; Phil. 3.9. Paul's genitives ('of' phrases) are often ambiguous, but they always connect the two words very closely, and as 'the faith of the gospel' at Phil. 1.27 is convincingly translated by REB as 'gospel faith', one might risk 'Jesus faith' here. Whether Paul has simply (Christian) believers in mind, or (as some now argue) the human response of Jesus himself to God, has to be decided in the light of one's total sense of Paul's theology. The obedient 'human Jesus' suggestion can appeal to Rom. 5.19 and Phil. 2.8, and it is attractive to some types of modern theology, but Paul's usual focus on the risen Lord makes the traditional view seem more likely to many. They still see insufficient exegetical reason for such a drastic revision of their historical pictures of the apostle's thought.

It is necessary to tread warily through these exegetical ambiguities and to recognize how our own beliefs may distort our reading of Paul. What he says about the death of Christ in vv. 25-26 carries a heavy doctrinal freight concerning the atonement. It is also obscure and open to different interpretations, depending above all on how 'God's righteousness' is understood. It is hard to doubt that Paul's unusual terminology and overloaded clauses in these verses stem from his quoting earlier liturgical formulae and perhaps commenting on them as he proceeds, but a closer look at this passage can wait until more of the jigsaw is in place (p. 90).

The weighty theological concepts of 1.17 have sometimes (wrongly) overshadowed Paul's simple and strongly emphasized point that the gospel leading to salvation is for everyone who believes, Jew first and Greek. Similarly 2.9-11 and 3.9 insisted that both groups are in the same plight. So, too, here it is important to give due weight to the 'no distinction' in 3.22. That Jews and Gentiles are in the same situation (all sinned, v. 23) and are righted in the same way is evidently important to Paul in Romans. What that way actually is (faith in or of Christ), and what it means for believers' lives, naturally receive most attention. But Paul was also interested in the similarity of Jews' and Gentiles' treatment by God, and his interest has to be explained historically and

theologically. His 'equal opportunities' campaign was not
motivated by modern ideas of equality.

Jews are righted 'from faith' and Gentiles 'through the
(that same) faith' (v. 30); the change of preposition may or
may not be rhetorical. God is God of Gentiles as well as of
Jews (v. 29). The 'boasting' that is excluded must mean
Jewish celebration of their covenant privileges, notably the
law. What Paul means by 'law of works' in contrast to 'law of
faith' is uncertain. Most read 'law' as 'principle' here, as at
7.21, 24, 8.2 and perhaps 9.31, but perhaps Paul is here
(3.27) contrasting the law as a narrative of faith (e.g. the
story of Abraham which follows) with the law as a system of
religious ritual (which is what the phrase 'works of the law'
seems to mean in the newly published Qumran material).

4.1-25
Chapter 3 ended with Paul's claim that (contrary to what we
might have expected) he 'establishes law' (presumably the
Jewish law or Torah). We might link that back to the positive
statements at 3.21b, or even 3.20b, or forward to ch. 4, or
find a deeper rationale at 8.4. The content of the law is God's
will; the only question is how that is obeyed. This v. 31 raises
again the theological question of Paul's view of the law. It
also contributes to the historical picture of Paul trying hard
to be positive about it while insisting that a right relationship to God comes not from Torah observance but from
Christ-faith. Both levels call for explanation and there is
always a chance that Paul's historical situation forced him
into theological contradictions, though we may be inclined to
give him the benefit of any doubt, as he was obviously not a
fool, and not obviously a knave.

The next chapter begins with some confusion among the
manuscripts as scribes were perhaps puzzled by Paul's
biblical echo 'found', but the whole chapter is evidently
intended to give scriptural support for Paul's central thesis
in 1.17 and 3.21-30. As in Galatians 3, Abraham is introduced as one whose right relationship with God was a matter
of his 'faith', and this is contrasted with the alternative possibility of being 'righted from works' (4.2). Gen. 15.6 is
the same key text that Paul used at Gal. 3.6 to associate

righteousness with believing. It is quoted in v. 3 and again in v. 9 (and is echoed in v. 22).

In view of what precedes (3.20-31), the point of this quotation must be to base righteousness on faith (cf. Phil. 3.9), not to say how this happened, namely by 'imputation' as orthodox Protestantism was to argue. The Greek verb 'calculated' or 'reckoned' (translated into Latin as *imputare* by Erasmus) came into Paul's discussion because it was there in Gen. 15.6—the only Septuagint verse apart from Hab. 2.4 (quoted earlier at 1.17) that links 'right' language with faith, or having faith.

But landed with this 'accounting' word Paul trades on it. A rabbinic exegetical rule (*gezĕrah sawa*) allows interpreters to bring in another text using the same word to illuminate the first. Paul can therefore quote Ps. 32 (LXX 31).1-2a which uses the same word and speaks furthermore of forgiveness of sins. This confirms incidentally that Paul's 'righteousness by faith' language speaks of a right relationship to God in the present. But the points he is making are those he has made in 3.21-30: (1) This is a matter of 'grace' (v. 4), that is, gift, not just deserts. 'Boasting' or feeling pleased with oneself is therefore misplaced. (2) It applies to those who are not circumcised, that is, Gentile believers, as much as to those who are circumcised (i.e. Jewish Christians), because Abraham was not yet circumcised at this point in the Genesis narrative.

The same point is made at Gal. 3.6-9, as part of an argument against Gentile converts receiving circumcision—though, as Abraham went on to do just that, this example seems damaging to Paul's case and was probably introduced by his judaizing opponents. Paul turns it to support his own case by arguing that it is believers who are Abraham's sons, all believers—and this is his point here, too (v. 11). Circumcision was merely a confirmatory sign or seal.

The Genesis text has introduced a shift from the earlier emphasis in 3.21-30 on *God's* righteousness righting believers and making them right or righted, to the *human* who is righted and can thus be credited with righteousness, that is, a right relationship with God. This is based on faith in a God (4.5) whose dealings with Abraham in his 'godless' state Paul sees as a prototype for his dealings with Gentiles

now. He can call it (in another pregnant genitive) 'righteousness of faith' (vv. 11-13), that is, 'faith righteousness', based
on God's gift alone and contrasted in v. 4 with something
earned or owed.

Much has been made of this 'working' and earning a
reward as though you could earn salvation. But neither Paul
nor any other Jews or Christians thought that salvation was
earned. The 'works' that some took pride in presumably
consisted in performing what God had given them in the law
to do, including circumcision, the sign of Israel's covenant
membership and their being sons of Abraham. Paul has not
quite said so directly, but it seems that he is contrasting a
relationship to God (sonship), based on faith in Jesus
Messiah, with one based on membership of the old covenant
people and characterized by observance of the law of Moses,
notably circumcision, and (cf. ch. 14) the food laws. (Sabbath
observance, an issue in Col. 2.16, is also possibly alluded to
at 14.6.)

The negative statement that right relationship to God does
not depend on law observance is now reinforced (as in Gal.
3.14-29) by contrasting law and faith with respect to the
promise made to Abraham, here in v. 13, that he would
inherit the world (cf. Gen. 18.18; 22.17-18). This promise
made Abraham father of many nations or Gentiles (Gen.
17.5, echoed in Rom. 4.17, 18). Abraham's response was
faith, and Paul relates Abraham's faith to Christian faith in
the risen Jesus both by echoing in v. 17 the Jewish Prayer of
18 Benedictions (Blessed art thou...who gives life to the
dead), and by seeing a kind of resurrection in the birth of
Isaac from Abraham's and Sarah's worn-out reproductive
organs.

The positive meaning of faith-righteousness and the application (v. 23) of this scriptural support are both clear and
explicit. The whole passage is rounded off with a couplet that
again looks like a quotation from the common Jewish-
Christian liturgical stock. It perhaps echoes the suffering
servant song (Isa. 53.4-5) that may have been the origin of
'righting' language in early Jewish Christianity (Isa. 53.11),
but this use of the word 'justification' as based on the resurrection in v. 25 is not quite how Paul himself elsewhere uses

this language, and that is an indication that he may be quoting from an existing Christian formulation.

Typical of Romans is the negative statement about the law in vv. 13-14 and the unnecessary reflection on its purpose in v. 15, as at 3.20b. Though Abraham is a positive illustration of faith and right relationship with God, Paul is clearly interested in the negative corollary, and it seems to worry him. He needs to explain to himself if to no one else why God gave a law which was to prove inadequate to its task of maintaining the right relationship within God's covenant with Israel. Paul's reply at 3.20, 4.15 and later at 5.20 and 7.7ff. gives the law a role, but a more ambiguous role than Jews generally assigned to this gift.

The end of ch. 4 looks like the end of a whole section of the epistle which began at 1.16. The subject in one word is 'righteousness', God's action in righting the world and humans' right relationship to God consisting in the appropriate response to this: the righting event is identified with the death and resurrection of 'Jesus Messiah our Lord', and the right relationship to God through him is called faith, which means trust, obedience, attachment to him. But from 3.20 on, this text was shot through with a subtext: that righteousness is not a matter of law observance. Since Paul has taken pains to underline his concern for morality, his 'not by works' probably refers to something else, and it seems from chs. 2 and 4 that circumcision, the sign of membership in the old covenant people of God, might be at issue. The importance of this subtext is confirmed by Paul's repeated emphasis on *all* believers, Jews and Gentiles, being in the same predicament, and being rescued in the same way, not by Torah observance but through Christ-faith.

That has now been argued from Scripture. The next four chapters are almost devoid of direct scriptural quotation, though 5.12-21 builds on the story of Adam, and 7.7-11 probably reflects on both Adam and on Moses and the law. After a transitional paragraph (vv. 1-11) which echoes the earlier language of being righted from faith (5.1) and the sacrificial death of Jesus (5.6-10) these terms are almost abandoned. After 5.2 faith and believing are not mentioned until 9.30ff.

apart from a weak use of the verb at 6.8. 'Righteousness' occurs at 5.17, 21 and 8.10, but in 6.13-20 it has a moral rather than a theological sense, as does 'righteous' at 5.7 and 7.12. Only 5.19 preserves the strong theological sense of relationship with God, though in biblical thought that distinction between religion and ethics is not sharp. The 'righting' verb occurs with a slightly different flavour at 6.7 before being picked up at 8.30, 33, and 'the just requirement of the law' is mentioned at 8.4, but that passage does not speak of justification, that is, being righted on a basis of faith.

Only the digression in 5.15-18 contains a patch of 'right' words looking back to God's righting act, and older analyses used to place ch. 5 with chs. 1–4 on justification. But other factors tie this transitional chapter more closely with what follows, especially the language of Christian existence which is introduced in 5.1-11 and unfolded in ch. 8.

These four chapters (5–8) hang together because they speak of Christian existence rather than the event which made that possible. As such they follow naturally from what preceded them and so encourage the view of Romans as a systematic account of Paul's gospel. But it has become clear that 1.16–4.25 was as much an argument as an exposition. It is therefore necessary to ask whether these chapters, too, are part of the same argument, and what exactly that argument might be.

The language of faith and righting almost disappears after ch. 5 until 9.30. But the subtext of chs. 1–4 concerning the law now becomes even more prominent. It intrudes unexplained at the end of ch. 5 and dominates ch. 7. Even chs. 6 and 8 touch obliquely on its significance because they speak of morality which is a large part of what the law is about, and which Paul's opponents had been critical of his gospel for supposedly undermining (3.8). Morality and the law are also both reflected in the new emphasis on the negative power called 'sin' in 5.12 and 8.3 (cf. 3.9). But the main thrust of chs. 5–8 lies in the positive state of affairs which is contrasted with this in ch. 8, where Christian existence is explicated.

How does that fit into the argument that 1.16–4.25 seemed to be developing against the necessity of Torah observance?

Galatians offers a possible parallel: before arguing from Scripture in Galatians 3–4 (cf. Rom. 4) for the thesis enunciated at Gal. 2.16 (cf. Rom. 3.21-28) about being righted on a basis of faith, Paul appeals in Gal. 3.1-5 to their experience of the Spirit. That itself is seen by Paul as sufficient proof that they are already in a right relationship with God, and so have no need of further adherence to the law of Moses. That might similarly be the point of Paul's account in chs. 5–8 of what it is to be a Christian. But first we must read and re-read these vital chapters.

The subdivisions of this section of Romans are clear and self-contained. Most of them are rounded off with a 'through Jesus Christ (or Christ Jesus) our Lord'. 5.1-11 becomes almost lyrical as it spells out the consequence of the salvation event reflected on in 1.1–4.25. Whether 'we *have* peace' or are exhorted to have it (the text is uncertain), 'peace' (Old Testament *shalom*) describes a relationship, here the relationship towards God implied also by Paul's 'righted from faith' language (v. 1). This is effected 'through our Lord Jesus Christ' who also made possible the believer's new standpoint. Paul labels it 'grace' or gift, and says it includes the joyful hope of 'glory'. Even the present sufferings (generally expected to be part of the end-time) can be celebrated for what they bring about: endurance, tested character, hope. God pours out love in our hearts through the gift of the Holy Spirit. This reveals God's love and gives grounds for future hope of salvation from judgment. Reconciliation, another model from human relationships, has already taken effect and carries with it the promise of future sharing in the risen life of Christ. It is therefore possible to rejoice in God 'through our Lord Jesus Christ'.

This celebration of what God has done for us in Christ is evoked by some highly rhetorical language that includes the note of pathos ('death of his Son', v. 10). The vicarious nature of Jesus' death is intended to draw a response and commitment from the believing hearer and to provide a strong religious backcloth to the arguments which follow.

5.12-21

These arguments begin with this subsection which seems
both transitional and pivotal. It reinforces the proclamation
of vv. 1-11 in a quite different and more argumentative style,
but it also introduces some of the ideas and symbols which
will dominate chs. 6–8, especially the overarching idea of
two contrasting spheres of influence, or power blocks. The
Adam story is briefly signalled (v. 12) and balanced by the
gospel story (v. 19), and the consequences of each are
contrasted. But this skeleton is fleshed out with digressions
(vv. 13-14, 15-18) and a comment about the law in v. 20
which is unexpected despite the references to the law in the
first digression (v. 13) where they mark a temporal and theological boundary.

The paragraph is thus weighty, but convoluted, and leaves
the reader uncertain about where the argument comes from
and is going. Despite the 'therefore' with which the paragraph begins, how it follows on from vv. 1-11 is not clear. The
references to sin, death and the law point back to chs. 1–4
and forward to the liberation from them discussed in chs.
6–8. There is no need to decide whether 'righteousness' in v.
21 refers primarily to God's saving act, as in 1.17 and 3.21, or
(as here in v. 17) to the God-given 'righteousness of faith'
(4.11 and 13), that is, the transformed human situation that
results from this divine intervention. Either way (and Paul
could have meant both) that key word forms a strong link
with the salvation and faith event of chs. 1–4 while also
introducing the main theme of chs. 5–8: believers' gifted life
as 'lived justification' within the rule of Christ.
'Righteousness' is still a theological term which includes but
it not exhausted by the moral dimension of the word that
surfaces in the next chapter. The essential point is that now
'Grace rules' where before 'Sin ruled', in a sphere or through
a power called Death, and that this rule of grace is leading to
'eternal life'—a phrase which will recur at the end of the next
chapter also (6.22, 23).

That is all heavily coded language, and a modern reader
needs to know the code before it makes much sense. But
anyone reading it can see at a first reading that a contrast is
being set up, and that the positive words—grace, Jesus,

Christ, righteousness, life—are contrasted with the nega-
tively weighted sin, death, Adam (named in v. 14 and implied
in vv. 12, 15-19, 'Adam' being Hebrew for 'human'). It is also
clear that the named individuals on both sides of the contrast
have mythic proportions. Both Adam and Christ have cosmic
effects. They are responsible for introducing into the world
sin or grace (cf. 1 Cor. 15.21). As a result all humans are
constituted sinners and that leads to death, or are constituted right, which leads to eternal life. Life and death are not
used simply in the literal biological sense here, though the
physical death of Adam and his successors is included in this
'death'. The further symbolic meaning of both these biological
terms is kept afloat by the less ordinary words in this religious language-game that is believed to mediate (not merely
describe) ultimate reality.

The second digression (vv. 15-18) works within the overarching contrast between two spheres ruled by personified
Sin and Grace respectively. It insists that the latter
outweighs the former. Paul is a monotheist, not a dualist—
God's gift of life must outgun the negative powers—but the
main point of the digression seems to be to reinforce the
contrasting spheres by some strong and resounding rhetoric.
It needs to be read aloud, preferably in Greek. The first
digression (vv. 13-14) is more substantial. The contrast
between Adam and Christ which controls the whole paragraph introduces the spatial idea of two realms. But Genesis
1–3 on which this contrast is based also introduces the
Bible's 'history of salvation' temporal model. Verse 13
comments on the temporal period between Adam and Moses
and it seems to Paul slightly anomalous.

But why does it seems anomalous to Paul? The close association of sin and death is taken from Genesis and posed no
problem for him, unlike his modern readers. Associating
death as well as sin with disobedience applied to Adam, but
not to his successors prior to Moses, since they did not have
God's command not to eat the forbidden fruit. Instead of
reverting to the Stoic natural theology used at 1.19-20 and
2.14-15 to insist that all are morally accountable, under sin,
and therefore subject to death, Paul treats the period
between Adam and Moses as an anomaly in which people

died despite having no direct divine command to break. Paul is not primarily concerned here with accountability and universal guilt, as he was in 1.18–3.18, though he may touch on that in the obscure phrase tacked on to v. 12. He is more concerned with its character as disobedience and so its close association with God's commandment, whether to Adam or through Moses. The mention of the law in vv. 13-14, and the abrupt introduction of the law in v. 20 are not so surprising as it first appears. Paul apparently wants to contrast grace, Jesus Christ and life with existence under the law—even if he is reluctant to say so directly.

That suspicion will be confirmed by 6.14 where Paul says, 'You are not under law but under grace'—rather than 'not under sin', as we should expect from the context. It seems that 'law' is being subtly (and shockingly) associated with sin, as a power which holds humanity in its grip and from which people need to be liberated.

6.1-23
This next subsection takes up the idea of Sin as a personified power, ruling over its own death-marked sphere (5.21, cf. 6.14). Paul contrasts the sphere of Sin with that of 'grace', and the moral aspect of sin with 'righteousness'. His argument is that believers have been freed from the power of Sin by a kind of death which released them from their citizenship of that realm, and that it is quite unthinkable for them to go on living as though they were still subject to that power. This chapter is simpler than the last because the spatial contrast between the realm of Sin on the one hand and that of Grace and righteousness on the other is here not complicated by a temporal contrast drawn from the biblical history of salvation. Even the Freudian slip noticed in v. 14, and the consequent discussion in v. 15, which echoes Paul's complicated interest in the law, remains in ch. 6 within the bounds of the spatial metaphor of a kingdom or great power's sphere of influence and domination.

Chapter 6 is neatly constructed to arise naturally out of what has just been said. The assertion that 'grace abounding' outweighs sin (5.20) might give rise to the suggestion that sin can be tolerated—an inference which 3.8 said some were drawing from Paul's teaching. Now that objection is answered. But we may ask in passing what gave rise to the accusation that Paul was soft on morality. The discursive style of this epistle suggests it was a logical inference drawn from his doctrine. But it was far more likely a natural concern stemming from his missionary practice. If Paul waived the Jewish Torah for his Gentile converts what constraints would remain on their behaviour? Again it seems that the controversy familiar to us from Galatians over whether Gentile converts need to observe Torah lies in the historical background to this epistle, even though no such controversy is mentioned.

Paul now answers this legitimate worry about morality. It was a legitimate concern, as morality was no longer guided and constrained by law observance. He provides a new basis for morality by appealing to the nature of Christian existence. Instead of the law's 'though shalt not' Paul says that believers' behaviour is (or should be) determined by who or what and where they are.

Again the language is heavily coded. Remaining in sin (v. 1) and dying to sin and living in it (v. 2) are not immediately intelligible phrases. Paul refers to the rite of initiation which his hearers have all undergone, and interprets it (and counts on their agreement—maybe this is not just his idea) as baptism 'into Christ Jesus' and 'into his death'. Some kind of symbolic identification with Jesus' destiny is attributed to the ritual act. It re-enacts his burial and the believer comes out of the water into a new moral life. Paul does not say (as Col. 3.1 does) that they were themselves already 'raised with Christ' after being 'buried with him through baptism into death' (v. 4) or 'co-planted in the likeness of his death' (v. 5), but he does say that Christ was raised and that Christian existence is determined by this: we live the new life and shall in the future share in that resurrection. Our old self was annihilated in this event, and so we no longer stand in the service of sin. Death, even this symbolic death (since the symbol mediates a reality more real than material reality), implies a break with the old ties and liberation from the power called Sin, even though life with Christ remains a matter for hope and the future (v. 8).

Christ's death and resurrection both motivate and
empower the Christian moral life. On the basis of their
identification with Christ believers are urged to reckon themselves 'dead to sin' (v. 11, cf. v. 2) and not let it rule them. A
contrast is drawn between (a) submitting oneself to the rule
of sin, which results in making oneself a tool in the hand of
wickedness, and (b) submitting oneself (as part of the new
age) to God. That (b) results in becoming weapons of 'righteousness'—here the contrast with wickedness gives 'righteousness' a moral meaning. What it means to be a believer is
described in terms of obedience to one rule or another and
the moral (or immoral) consequences that flow from that.

The subtle switch from being 'under sin' to being 'under
the law' suggests that Paul's concern is not with the basis of
Christian morality as such, but with its basis when the law
is no longer in place to motivate and guide behaviour. In v.
16 he reverts to the contrast between the powers of Sin
(leading to death) and obedience (which is virtually synony-
mous with faith, cf. 1.5 and 16.19, 26) leading 'to righteousness'—both the theological meaning (right relation with God)
and the ethical (right behaviour) are present in v. 16. The
metaphor of being enslaved to one power or to another is
continued by Paul's speaking paradoxically of liberation from
sin into a new 'slavery', namely to serve righteousness. He
acknowledges that he is speaking metaphorically (v. 19) to
make his point. But he really does think of morality in terms
of purity and impurity, and here he introduces the notion of
'sanctification' or holiness of life. The moral vocabulary of
'righteousness' (five times in this chapter, vv. 13-20), and the
domination and slavery metaphors, are fused with this new
moral vocabulary found elsewhere in Paul (holy life in
1 Thess. 4, and the purity motif most strongly in
1 Corinthians). This ethical thrust points to the final reward,
eternal life—or conversely death, the wage that Sin pays.

These are not merely future states. Those who are baptized
'into' Christ Jesus (v. 3) already enjoy life 'in' (or through)
Jesus Christ our Lord (v. 23), and that life in Christ is the
basis of Christian ethics. It will be further unfolded in ch. 8.

Paul's account of this implies an anthropology or view of
the human condition, and one which contradicts modern

ideas of autonomy. The slavery metaphor is applied, even though with a grain of salt, to a Christian existence that is also described in terms of freedom, as in Galatians. This 'freedom of a Christian', most powerfully described in Luther's 1520 treatise with that title, is orientation to a new Lord, a new power 'whose service is perfect freedom'. Whether it is legitimate to draw from this metaphor doctrinal consequences about the human will not being free is a further question best deferred until Romans 7 and 9 have been studied.

7.1-6

'In Christ Jesus our Lord' (6.23, cf. 5.11, 21) marks the end of a paragraph, but the next chapter is closely linked. 'Or do you not know' echoes 6.3, and begins a more difficult section. The three paragraphs of 7.7-25 draw back from the shocking implications of vv. 1-6. The illustration drawn from marriage law (vv. 2-3) relates what is said here to the previous chapter. The fit is not exact, but again a death brings liberation. Only now it is liberation not from the power of Sin but from the law.

That close association of sin and the law is sufficiently shocking for Paul to deny any actual identification between them (v. 7) and to say some positive things about the law. But his general point stands. The woman is 'free from the law' (v. 3) and Paul tells his hearers that they too 'were done to death to the law through the body of Christ, so as to belong to someone else'. In other words they are free from the law and belong to the risen Christ. The death that has brought this about is his death—the 'body of Christ' surely refers to his crucified body.

That does not contradict 6.3. Baptism effects a symbolic identification of the believers with Christ but it is still the death and resurrection of Christ that is the foundation of Christian existence. The moral fruit of that is again touched on (vv. 4-5) as are the slavery metaphor (v. 6) and the contrast of life and death. The previous chapter is thus briefly recapitulated, but a new vocabulary for the contrast is introduced in v. 6: the old and the new are contrasted as letter and Spirit. That familiar contrast was used slightly

differently in 2.29. A closer parallel is 2 Cor. 3.6. The 'letter'
or written code is clearly the Jewish law.

The full unfolding of the new life in Christ as life in the
Spirit follows in ch. 8. It will take up and develop themes
introduced in 5.1-11 and is clearly the climax of this section
of the epistle (chs. 5-8). The contrast drawn in 7.6, however,
suggests that Paul's point is not simply to clarify Christian
existence, but to contrast it with life under the law. That
would fit Paul's general intention noted here and in chs. 1–4
to argue that believers are not subject to the law of Moses.
But in contrast to Galatians, Paul is being as positive as he
can be about the law, short of abandoning his claim that it is
not what being a believer is essentially about, and that
therefore Gentile converts need not be circumcised or observe
the food laws.

That is Paul's sticking point and it allows no room for
compromise. But he remains convinced that it is God's law,
expresses God's will and promises the inclusion of Gentiles
with the coming of messiah. It is absurd to call the law sin—
though Paul has come dangerously close to this. He now
clarifies his position. The law had or has a purpose in making
sin known, but Sin (still a personified power) used it to cause
havoc in a humanity prone to disobedience. The problem lay
in human moral weakness (cf. 8.3) which was bound to capit-
ulate to Sin by disobeying the law once we knew it. So the
problem was not the law (in principle a good thing) but the
conjunction of weak human nature, the power of Sin, and the
command that gave Sin its chance.

7.7-23
The exegetical debates about this subsection (vv. 7-25) have
focused on the identity of the 'I', and it was once widely
thought that Paul was writing autobiographically. This
allowed readers to see him in terms of Luther's experience
with its roots in Augustine and medieval piety and its shoots
in subsequent Protestant pietism. That led some to propose
psychological theories to explain Paul's conversion. But there
is no evidence that prior to his conversion he was tormented
over keeping the law (cf. Phil. 3.6), and these verses are now
widely understood in the light of 7.6 as describing the old,

pre-Christian existence under the law—not as it appeared to Paul at the time, but as it appears to him now. The 'I' is more general than autobiographical, as is suggested by the possible allusions here again to the Adam (= human) story that was already introduced at 5.12-21 (cf. 7.11, sin 'deceived' me, with Gen. 3.13).

The ambiguity which conceals this allusion to Genesis 1–3 in vv. 7-11 is that here as in ch. 5 it is conflated with a reference to the law given to Moses. The tenth commandment is rightly quoted as 'the law' speaking. But this commandment is reminiscent of the Adam story, and that allusion is confirmed by the death which is said in v. 10 to follow (cf. Gen. 2.17; 3.3, 19).

Paul is wanting to avoid blaming the law. It is holy and spiritual, and (God's) commandment is holy, right and good (vv. 12, 14). Sin is to blame—and human nature, or the human condition, which is 'fleshly'. The ordinary word 'flesh' carries symbolic or theological weight for Paul, as is apparent from 7.5. It can be used neutrally to refer to human mortality, in contrast to God's Spirit (cf. Isa. 31.3), but the contrast with God's Spirit is used by Paul especially in Rom. 8.3-13 and Galatians 5 to describe human existence under the power of sin, in contrast to Christian existence which is life in the Spirit.

In v. 14 this 'I' is said to be sold under the power of Sin, and in view of the account of Christian existence in ch. 6 as freedom from sin that must surely signify pre-Christian existence. But all that then follows could very well describe most Christians' ordinary moral experience, and it has often been taken that way. The identity of the 'I' is perhaps less important for understanding vv. 14-25 than for vv. 7-13. Paul's account of the divided person looks like an exploration of the human situation, and it has generated profound reflections on this. But the argument in Romans thus far would lead us to expect Paul to be wanting to deny that the ritual demands of the law apply to Christians. Where he wants his argument to lead is clear in 8.2-3—freedom from a law which, on account of dislocated human existence (flesh), could not help. Instead of being negative about the Jewish law, as he is in Galatians 3, Paul draws on a commonplace of human experience found also in the Roman poet Ovid: 'I see the better, and approve; but I do the worse'. This allows Paul to be positive about God's law while insisting on the need for redemption. The human will is trapped and needs the rescue which Christ and the Spirit bring.

This recourse to a moral commonplace leads Paul to contrast 'mind' and 'flesh' in a dualistic way. That is untypical, but philosophical consistency was not Paul's concern. 'The inner man' (v. 22) is also here used in a way less typical of Paul's anthropology than at 2 Cor. 4.16. It is possible to draw a doctrine of the enslaved will from these verses, but that was scarcely Paul's concern either. He was surely contrasting life lived under the law with the new life in the Spirit (7.6). He wants to be negative about the former without being negative about God's law as such. Having come perilously close to calling the law itself sin by associating them so closely as powers from which we have to be liberated, he now takes a different tack. He takes advantage of the double meaning of *nomos* (law) which can also mean 'principle'. Paul's usual meaning, the law of Moses which is God's law, is never far away, and 'the law of my mind' in v. 23 presumably refers to or includes the law of God (v. 22) that I consent to. The 'other law in my members' (v. 23), closely associated or identified with 'the law of sin which is in my members' (v. 23) is perhaps best translated vaguely as 'principle', as in v. 21. It refers to the human situation as subject to the power of sin and heading for death (v. 24).

Whether or not Paul intended this, what he says here has been reflected in the experience of many believers. They remain subject to the constraints and distortions of physical existence even if no longer oriented to these, and look forward to bodily redemption. The new truth about their lives makes them more sensitive to the ambiguities that remain, whereas those who remain at home in the old norms may experience less discomfort.

7.24–8.11

The good news affirmed at the beginning of ch. 8 underlines the reply given in 7.25a to the cry of pain in 7.24, but it does not exclude that cry being made by believers (cf. 8.23). They can yearn for rescue even while knowing they are not condemned. But if, as is possible, these verses do include Christian experience, then Paul's rhetoric has in 7.21-25 carried him away from his theme of freedom from the law. Indeed in v. 25b he serves God's law, at least with his mind, corresponding to the positive comments in vv. 7ff., especially v. 16. That may seem hard to reconcile with not requiring circumcision of his Gentile converts. It encourages some scholars to cut 7.25b out as a gloss. But v. 25b goes no further than v. 16 (which is not taken to be a gloss), and 1 Cor. 7.19 can also surprisingly contrast circumcision with the commands of God (cf. Gal. 6.15). Paul can think of God's moral will expressed in the law without including circumcision because he starts from his present convictions about God's will, not from the law as such.

The calculated ambiguity about the law, noted at 3.27 and present in 7.23, is also found in the opening verses of ch. 8. Nomos is to be translated 'principle', twice in 8.2, even though in v. 3 the word, as usual in Paul refers to the Torah. Two 'principles' are contrasted: Spirit which is life 'in' Christ Jesus is contrasted with sin and death, which are closely connected. But the association of law (the Torah) with sin and death in chs. 5–7 resonates in the second part of 8.2 also. A shadow is thrown over Torah by the double entendre, and this is confirmed by v. 3 which refers to the impotence of Torah. Here the saving event is spoken of as God's 'sending' his Son (as at Gal. 4.4—and especially John's Gospel), and in sacrificial language. 'Concerning sin' is probably an echo of Septuagint usage, meaning 'as a sacrifice for sin' (cf. Lev. 4.14; 5.6-7; etc.). The inability of the law to help is explained by reference to the dislocated human condition (flesh) as taught in the previous chapter, and God has passed sentence on sin in the human realm shared by Jesus. The purpose and result of all this is said to be that the law's righteous demand can be fulfilled among believers (8.4).

These few verses are quite dense. Paul says or alludes to a great deal in a few rhetorical phrases. His short shafts call for long explanations. The most striking remark for readers noticing how preoccupied Paul seems to be with the question of the law is that its right or just requirement is assumed to be fulfillable and fulfilled by those who 'walk according to Spirit' (v. 4).

That theological category has a moral content. The flesh–Spirit contrast among humans results in contrasting behaviour. One mindset means reconciliation with God (life and peace), the other hostility towards God, an unwillingness and inability to obey and please God, resulting in death. But you believers, says Paul, are not in *that* sphere (in flesh) but *this* (in Spirit)—if God's Spirit dwells in you (v. 9). That is apparently the same as the Spirit of Christ (v. 9b), and the mark of belonging to him. And the Spirit of Christ is no different from the risen Christ himself. So Christ is 'in' believers (cf. Gal. 2.20) and though their body is dead (heading for dissolution) on account of sin, the Spirit is life (cf. v. 2) on account of (God's?) righteousness, probably God's saving action, or a right relationship with God, rather than the human moral virtue which ensues. The close connection between God's Spirit and the resurrection of Jesus (cf. 1.4) means that God will by his indwelling Spirit give life to the mortal bodies that the Spirit indwells.

8.12-17
As at 6.12-14, so here (8.12-13), Paul draws moral conse-quences from his theological affirmations. His ethic is a Spirit ethic in the sense that the Spirit is a realm that believers inhabit and a power that guides and directs them, contrasting with the realm and downward pull of 'flesh' or human nature dislocated by Sin. The consequences of these contrasting orientations are again life or death. A character-istic of life in the Spirit is 'sonship', an intimate relationship to God expressed in prayer (v. 15), as in the Lord's Prayer which probably began Abba, Father (cf. Lk. 11.2; also Gal. 4.6 and Mk 14.36).

Spirit is an ambiguous word which can refer to the powerful activity of God or (in Greek usage) to the immate-rial part of humans which inhabits the body. Paul thinks of humans more holistically, but can speak as here (v. 10) of 'our spirit', meaning humans in their receptivity to God. As in ch. 4 the notion of sonship (there the seed of Abraham) introduces the idea of 'heirs', but here it is the relationship with God and Christ that is discussed, a relationship that involves present sufferings and future (resurrection) glory (v. 17).

8.18-25
That future, eschatological dimension of Christian existence is discussed next. It provides the context for understanding the present sufferings of both believers and the wider creation. The world has been subjected to futility or meaninglessness and awaits rebirth. The end of the old age had been expected to include tribulations—the birthpangs of the new—and believers were not excluded from these. Hope is their watchword as they wait for God's glory to be revealed, and for the creation's rescue from bondage and decay. That transition into the glorious liberty of the children of God will be the completion of believers' own redemption.

8.26-39
Meanwhile the Spirit gives a foretaste, supporting believers in their weakness, teaching them to pray aright, and interceding on their behalf. And so the passage rises into a crescendo and finally doxology. Such purple passages as Romans 8 can never be adequately paraphrased. It is enough to note the emphasis on loving God (v. 28), God's call and foreknowledge and conformity to the image of his Son, the brief recurrence of 'righting' language (vv. 30, 33), the echo of the binding of Isaac (he spared not his own son, v. 32), the death, resurrection and heavenly session of Jesus, the love of Christ, God's love for us, the love of God that is in (or through) Christ Jesus our Lord. Paul's rhetoric communicates before it is understood. Many who understand little of his theology know from this chapter what it means to be a Christian.

Chapters 9–11

The tone changes dramatically as a new section begins in ch. 9. Its connection with what precedes is not obvious, but there are links with the story of Abraham in ch. 4. The exaltation of ch. 8 gives way to pathos—and then to scriptural argument. But why should Paul have to protest his grief

about Israel and his readiness like Moses to be cut off from
Christ on their behalf?

Presumably his loyalty as a Jew was suspect among Jews,
including Jews who accepted Jesus as messiah—as well it
might be if he were saying that circumcision and food laws
were unimportant. Writing to *all* believers in Rome (1.7),
including Jewish-Christians who did not know him personally, and hoping to win their support, he would have had to
address their suspicions and reservations. Protestations of
concern are no substitute for theological argument, but they
might help, and there is no reason to doubt Paul's sincerity.

He insists he values his kinsfolk Israel. Theirs are not only
God's earlier initiatives and the fathers, to whom Paul has
already appealed, but the earthly descent of the messiah
himself. Whatever Paul's position on the law, he was no
Marcion (below p. 133). Even apart from his own warm feel-
ings as a Jew, the Jewish tradition and experience are necessary if the gospel is from the Jewish God—blessed be
God—and concerns the Jewish messiah.

Paul's continual prayer for his fellow Jews, and his readiness to be cut off from Christ on their behalf (cf. Exod. 32.32)
indicates that the problem is their rejection of Christ. But it
is not quite so clear what kind of a problem that is. Verses 2-
3 refer to Paul's personal grief, but v. 6 suggests rather a
theological problem which must now be faced: has the word
of God failed?

The question whether the unbelief of some Jews has made
a nonsense of God's faithfulness (i.e. to the covenant between
God and Israel) was raised at 3.1-4. It was brushed aside at
that point. The issue is now treated at length, which shows
that it was a serious question. The earlier context may throw
light on it. There it was not a matter of Paul's personal feel-
ings, neither was it raised as a merely theoretical problem
about the character and effectiveness of God. The issue arose
in the context of what has begun to look like Paul's defence of
his missionary practice of not requiring Gentile converts to
be circumcised. It was perhaps this that led him to suggest
that literal circumcision was not the mark of a true Jew
(2.25). But that did not imply that the whole history and
tradition of Israel was now irrelevant. The 'oracles of God'

(3.2) are still essential, and Paul must therefore show how they cohere with his understanding of the gospel. He must make sense of Israel's history in God's plan, while continuing to assert that a right relationship to God is now to be found in Christ-faith, not by observance of Torah. So Gentiles need not be circumcised, he implies.

These chapters are therefore integral to the argument which it seems Paul is quietly pressing throughout the epistle. It is hardly the 'climax' of the argument, because the argument is not built up step by step. The case for Gentiles not needing to be circumcised (because a right relationship to God is to be found *this* way—by Christ-faith—not *that* way of Torah observance) is insinuated rather than stated directly. This section repeats Paul's theological warrants for his missionary practice: righteousness is from faith, not works. It does not aim to promulgate new doctrines (e.g. predestination or universalism), but neither does it merely answer an objection to Paul's theory of Christianity. Like what he says about morals, it is central to the structure of what he believes. Neither morality nor 'salvation-history' is the key to the Gospel of Christ, or the 'centre' of Paul's theology. Individuals' faith in Christ constitutes a relationship to God in Spirit within a Christian community. That is what the gospel brings about and it forms the centre from which theological reflection and moral life radiate. But Paul could not think of God without thinking of God's plan and action in history, any more than he could think of life in Christ or life in the Spirit without thinking of appropriate behaviour and prayer. In that sense what he says in these chapters is integral to his theological thinking and foundational to any theological sketches his readers might construct from the theological vocabulary of his scriptural echoes, doxologies and arguments.

But all that is to project an angle of vision from what has preceded in chs. 1–8. It must be tested by reading chs. 9–11. The main subdivisions are clear: 9.6-29; 9.30–10.21; 11.1-36. They do not yield a clear line of argument; ch. 11 may even contradict ch. 9. We must be ready for a series of arguments, and see how they relate to what is emerging as the general argument of the epistle.

As with ch. 4, the most striking feature of these chapters is their intensive quotation of Scripture. As in Galatians 3, things are being *argued* on a basis of Scripture and, as usual with Paul, when the argument is obscure it is best to look at the end and see where he was trying to get.

9.6-29

The first argument is clear: not all empirical Israel is truly Israel (9.7). The unbelief of some (3.2) is therefore not decisive. It is the children of the promise who are God's children—Isaac and his seed (cf. Gen. 18.10, 14), Jacob and his seed (Gen. 25). God's choice or election was made when the twins were in Rebecca's womb, so it was not based on anything they had done ('works'). All that shows that God is in control (v. 16) and was responsible for the pattern of Israel's faith which Paul and his hearers take for granted. But it seems unfair, and while Paul brushes the suggestion aside (9.14, cf. 3.5), we must ask why he pursues a line of thought that has caused such offence to his liberal and humane readers and commentators, from Origen to C.H. Dodd, who protested that 'man is not a pot'.

The answer may lie in Paul's introduction of Pharaoh and the Exodus (v. 17). The quotation of Exod. 9.16 and echo of Exod. 4.21 reflect general Jewish understanding of these events—God set Pharaoh up to knock him down—'so that (God's) name should be proclaimed in all the world' adds the text, very helpfully to Paul, the Gentile missionary. The argument might make an Anglican or an Erasmus wince, but Jews and Calvinists who accept the story in Exodus with its rather arbitrary view of God's sovereignty can hardly object to having it turned against themselves. Paul drives the argument home with echoes from the prophets, especially Isaiah (29.16; 45.9) which will provide much of the material in these three chapters.

The vocabulary and offensive ideas are biblical, but Paul's essential point is his own (v. 24): (God) called us, not only out of Jews, but also out of Gentiles (cf. Hos. 2.23; 1.10). A new people of God, consisting of Jews and Gentiles, is being constituted (cf. Gal. 6.16?; 1 Cor. 10.32). Only a remnant of empirical Israel will be saved (cf. Isa. 10.22-23), but that is something (cf. Isa. 1.9).

9.30–10.4

In the debating style familiar from chs. 2–3 ('what then?')
Paul draws a conclusion (9.30-32) from what precedes and at
the same time begins a new section. He re-introduces the
language of righteousness, faith and works that dominated
chs. 1–4 (and 5) and ties them to the question now under
discussion. In contrast to (some) Gentiles who have accepted
the gospel, Israel (as a whole) has rejected it. Obscure and
elliptical though his formulations are, the basic contrast is
clear. Gentiles have attained 'righteousness' without
pursuing it, whereas Israel has not, and the reason is that
righteousness is 'from faith' not works, that is, Torah observance. The 'stone' passages in Isa. 8.14 and 28.16 are
combined to encapsulate both the problem and the solution.
Jesus is identified as the stone (as in the use of Ps. 118.22-23
in Mk 12.10-11 and parallels), and faith in him is what is
needed. For those who reject him he is a stone they stumble
over. 'Righteousness' here must mean a right relationship to
God in the present. That implies membership of what in
1 Cor. 11.25 Paul and his tradition can call 'the new
covenant'. 'People of God' language is common in these chapters, but the emphasis remains on God and the faith-rela-
tionship to God rather than on the community of faith.
Righteousness also has future eschatological consequences,
but these are not mentioned here. It is the present situation
that concerns Paul, and grieves him.

Formally the new chapter begins a new section (10.1) with
a similar expression of distress to 9.2, but materially the
'righteousness' language of vv. 3-4, continued in the scriptural support in vv. 5ff., links it with 9.30-32. Here it is the
righteousness of God which leads to salvation, and that is
contrasted with their 'own righteousness' which Israel has
misguidedly preferred. Misguidedly, according to Paul,
because Christ is the end or goal of law, resulting in 'righteousness' for everyone who has faith (in him). 'Law' in v. 4 is
relativized by its reference to Christ, but pointing to him is a
relatively positive function. Unlike 'works of the law' it is not
here contrasted with God's righteousness, despite the
context.

Again, 'righteousness' is the key word and it refers to a

relationship to God in the present. Although 'faith' has a strong implication of individual responsibility Paul is still arguing in terms of groups: unbelieving Jews and Gentile believers. In vv. 5-6 he contrasts two ways of being related to God, Torah observance and faith (in Christ), and in v. 5 uses a quotation from Moses in Lev. 18.5 (also used at Gal. 3.12) to characterize the first. Law is a matter of doing it.

10.5-21
The alternative is elucidated by a more complicated piece of midrashic commentary on Deut. 30.12-14. Christ is present in Christian preaching. The response of faith in him will bring salvation. The language of (present) 'righteousness' is again parallelled with that of (future) salvation (vv. 9-10, cf. v. 1). Confessing Jesus as Lord and believing in his resurrection leads to a right relationship with God now and salvation in the future. Both stem from faith. Again Paul insists that this applies to all believers: there is no distinction between Jew and Gentile, because Christ is Lord of all, generous to all who call on him (cf. 3.22, 29). Calling on him stems from believing on him and that stems from hearing, which requires preaching, which requires mission. The gospel is acclaimed in a quotation of Isa. 52.7 better known to modern readers from Handel. But not all (!) believed, that is, were obedience to it (cf. Isa. 53.1). However, the words (of missionaries) went out into all the ends of the inhabited world (*oecumene*)—a quotation from Ps. 19.4. Israel might not believe, but God has this plan: a quotation from Deut. 32.21 in v. 19 introduces a new and extraordinary idea to be developed in the next chapter. Gentiles' acceptance of the gospel will make Israel jealous, and so respond. It will be God's way of bringing Israel in. Meanwhile, as Isa. 65.1-2 says, God is found among (Gentiles) who were not looking or asking for him, whereas Israel was disobedient.

11.1-36
Chapter 11 makes a fresh start, asking bluntly whether God rejected his people, and again protesting Paul's loyalty to Israel. Again the language of Scripture carries the argument, indicating that God's plan was all worked out in advance.

First the remnant idea, appealed to at 9.27-29 (Isa. 10.22-23; 1.9) is re-introduced by reference to the time of Elijah. Now as then there is 'a remnant based on (God's) choice and grace' (11.5), and that means 'not any longer from works' (v. 6). Again the antithesis which has haunted the epistle since ch. 3 is highlighted. What Israel was looking for (cf. 9.31), only the chosen hit on. The rest were 'hardened'—and again a string of quotations from Isaiah, Deuteronomy and the Psalms.

The rest of the chapter has much less biblical quotation, and even that is confirmatory (vv. 26-27) and doxological (vv. 34-35). The argument is more directly Paul's own, and it is remarkable. He claims that Israel's rejection of the gospel has brought salvation to the Gentiles and that this is intended to make Israel jealous (v. 11, cf. 10.19). He clearly envisages 'all Israel' finally coming in, and although he does not say coming to faith in Christ, 'the deliverer' of Isa. 59.20 quoted in v. 26 presumably refers to him. Addressing Gentile believers, presumably in Rome but possibly elsewhere as well (v. 13), Paul reiterates his hope that his Gentile mission will bring in some of his fellow Jews by this indirect route. His analogy of the wild olive representing Gentiles being grafted into the people of God warns them not to feel superior to the Jewish people. They too could fall and be cut off—and the original branches will be grafted back on if they do not remain in unbelief.

Finally Paul calls his theory about the Jews' eventual reconciliation a 'mystery' (v. 25). Their 'hardening' is only temporary, lasting until the full complement of Gentiles has come in. Then 'all Israel' will be saved. Their choice or 'election' by God has not been annulled. The reversal of roles that brings Gentiles in and puts Israel out will be overcome as they too are drawn into the mercy of God. The theory leads Paul into a Scripture-based doxology.

This chapter has proved a welcome resource for Jewish-Christian dialogue over the past generation and has been made the basis for theories which it is hard to conceive of Paul approving. Any interpretation that removes Christ from the centre of Paul's Jewish belief in God is incredible, and yet Christ is not directly mentioned in this chapter. Here Paul addresses a problem that is both theoretical and personal. Considering what it took to persuade Paul himself that Jesus is the messiah he cannot have been surprised by the common Jewish rejection of the gospel. It must have been all part of God's plan.

Accepting this understanding of what God was doing involved Paul in standing his earlier beliefs on their head. Once convinced about the crucified and risen messiah he might find reasons of a kind for God giving a law whose validity was only for a period. But it would have been surprising had many other Jews agreed with him. Were they then doomed? And if so, what price God's promises to the fathers? These chapters give different answers, and the last one is a bold and unverifiable theory: Israel might be impressed by what they see of Gentiles' participation in God's gift.

Subsequent history has done little to make this theory credible. Paul was willing to wait for eschatological verification, and in the meantime to remain optimistic. These chapters provide an answer to those who thought him a disloyal Jew. But the reason for their suspicion was his law-free Gentile mission. That is presupposed, not defended, in these chapters. It is therefore implausible to make Romans 9–11 the climax of the epistle, as though God's plan in history were the focus of his gospel. Rather, it was the backdrop of his gospel of Christ, and an optimistic backdrop that looks forward to the salvation of both Gentiles and Jews.

Chapters 12–16

The remainder of the epistle is more simple. It can be summarized here briefly and taken up in chs. 3 and 5. The heavily theological sections of Romans, chs. 1–4 (or 5), 5–8, 9–11, are now followed by moral exhortations and instruction (12–14) leading into more personal directions and information (15) and concluding greetings and doxology (16). The moral exhortations would follow more naturally on chs. 5–8 than 9–11, just as 9–11 would have fitted well after 1–4. Paul's ethics are grounded in his theological account of Christian existence and summed up in the language of worship. Morality is seen in terms of a sacrifice, without blood, involving self-offering to God and leading to renewal and moral discernment (12.1-2). The unity of the community is a main concern of ch. 12, as it is of 1 Corinthians 12 which is echoed here, and love is the key to Christian living, as in 1 Corinthians 13 (cf. also Rom. 14.15). Jesus' injunction to love our enemies is reflected in the echo of the synoptic tradition in v. 14 (cf. Mt. 5.44), but given a dangerous twist from Prov. 25.21-22 in v. 20. The pacifism of Jesus becomes more militant in v. 21, without becoming military.

The desperately influential advice to submit to the political authorities (13.1-7) seems out of place in an ethical context generally guided by love. It is explicable in view of Paul's eschatological expectations, echoed at 13.11, and the benefits of the Roman peace to his mission at the time he wrote, during Nero's five good years. The love command at 13.9-10 speaks only of loving the neighbour (Lev. 19.18) but it epitomizes the whole law, as in Gal. 5.14. Expectation of the end motivates behaviour, but more as a christological carrot than a stick (v. 14).

Chapter 14 discusses a practical problem in Christian common life and gives guidance for dealing with it. Christian freedom gives place to the claims of love. If believers are oriented to their Lord other issues are relativized. Paul makes his own liberal convictions about matters of ritual purity clear, but he will not allow these to destroy a fellow Christian. The aim is to build up a common life. The unusual use of 'faith' in vv. 22-23 is best translated 'conviction' (so REB, NRSV margin).

The contrast between those with weak and those with robust consciences (cf. 14.1) is continued into ch. 15, and again the principles of Christian behaviour are attractively presented. Christ is appealed to as an example as well as the foundation of a new realm of behaviour. Both these chapters raise the question of how much Paul knew about and was addressing problems of believers in Rome. The ecumenical thrust of 15.6-7 is striking, and its integration with the dominant theme of Jews and Gentiles in the church makes hypotheses about the local situation in Rome worthy of serious consideration, as we shall see in the next chapter.

The ministry of Christ to the circumcision (15.8) is said to confirm the promises to the fathers which Paul has built on in ch. 4, and worried about in chs. 9–11. That the Gentiles should glorify God for his mercy is celebrated in another string of biblical quotations from Ps. 18.49, Deut. 32.43, Ps. 117.1 and Isa. 11.10. In each of these passages the keyword is Gentiles (or nations) and the point of them all is Gentiles coming to worship God. They are rounded off with a blessing (v. 13) which could have ended the epistle. But it does not. Paul abruptly changes tone in v. 14 from the elegant style of the preacher to the down to earth correspondent, almost apologizing for his presumption in haranguing them. But, as at 1.8-13, his tact is tempered by his apostolic self-consciousness. He describes his own work in religious, even hierophantic, terms (v. 16) as offering the Gentiles as a sacrifice to God. Modesty is not appropriate here, simply factual reporting. Yet this is not simple description. He sees his representative preaching and establishing churches around the Eastern Mediterranean as having enormous significance. The Gentile mission must continue, so having completed his work in the East he is ready to go to Spain, via Rome. But first there is an important matter to be seen to in Jerusalem. The collection he has been raising in Greece must be delivered, and Paul clearly attaches great importance to it. He is also apprehensive about it and asks for their prayers—both for his safety and his enterprise there.

All this will prove significant when we try to determine Paul's purpose in writing. It poses fewer hermeneutical problems than the rest of the epistle. The same is true of ch. 16. Paul commends Phoebe and adds a surprisingly long list of greetings. Some have doubted whether this chapter was originally destined for Rome, and there is some textual evidence to support these doubts (see p. 155). But on most views of his purpose(s) it is intelligible that Paul should seek to maximize his contacts in Rome. Social historians find all this informative, but a first reading can afford to skim it. The doxology (16.25-27), placed earlier in some manuscripts and omitted in others, is untypical of Paul and may have been added later.

This part of the Guide has been almost as dense as Paul himself, though less ambiguous. Anyone who has absorbed it is already in a position to progress to a weightier commentary. Most users may have been more selective. The idea is to return to it after reading more of what follows, and find it gradually illuminating more of the epistle.

3

WHY DID PAUL
WRITE TO ROME?

UNLIKE MOST LITERATURE, letters presuppose an actual situation and some knowledge of it shared by the author and addressees. Reconstructing this from the letter itself and from external evidence is often vital for understanding a text that hinges on the writer's aims and relationship to the original recipients. Later readers draw on their general and specific knowledge and experience to feel their way into the original situation, and interpret what is said accordingly. Sometimes what is *not* said is important, and *how* things are said may reflect the subtleties and ambiguities involved in human relationships. A letter written in a foreign language long ago thus becomes intelligible to later readers who share (or can come to share) enough of its world to understand what is going on.

More than common sense, sensitivity and historical and linguistic knowledge is needed when the letter's realm of discourse is more specialized. A letter from Einstein telling a colleague of his discovery may be clear in aim, but opaque to later readers whose mathematical skills are limited. Identifying the subject matter as mathematics not Chinese is a start, and the author as a man to take seriously, too, but more technical knowledge is needed to understand that letter, not more knowledge of the author or recipient.

Paul's subject matter is less technical than Einstein's, but his language takes some mastering. He seems to speak of common human experience, and yet to use the language of his own quite particular religious tradition. Understanding the main body of the epistle is more difficult than understanding Paul's travel plans or his greetings, or even his moral admonitions. A further complication is that how we evaluate Paul's religious language may affect how we understand it. These different types of judgment are less separable in life than in logic.

Paul did not expect to be read centuries later, but he intended to say things that are generally true, not limited to some particular context. One might argue that the inclusion of his letters in the biblical canon does justice to that intention by weakening their links with their original contexts and strengthening their universal claim. However, their new context changes their texture, as the molten lava of Paul's religious discourse hardens in the settled categories of later doctrine. These may provide the best guides for reading the text, but critical modern readers are unlikely to take that on trust. They are more likely to want to reconstruct the original context in the hope of catching the original impulse and perhaps resolving some of the theological disputes surrounding this text. That involves respecting the 'occasional' character of Romans, that is, attending to the evidence of how it was 'occasioned' by particular circumstances. This is less obvious than in Galatians or 1 Corinthians, but even Romans can be viewed through a historical lens, as it was by F.C. Baur, who in 1836 asked about its 'purpose and occasion'. That line of enquiry distances the text and may alter our relationship to it. Historical contextualization is unlikely to provide the only key to a classic of religious literature. It may even seem to trivialize its majestic arguments and theological themes. But it promises to throw some light on a difficult ancient letter, and is therefore irresistible.

Paul's Plans

We know a lot about Paul and a little about Christianity in Rome from other sources, apart from what this epistle itself reveals. Six or more of his other letters survive, all written from about this time, probably over the previous eight years.

Acts was probably written a generation or so later but (to judge from cross-checking with the epistles) it seems broadly reliable about some of Paul's movements in the 50s. An inscription showing that Gallio was Proconsul in Corinth c. 50/51 (cf. Acts 18.12) provides some basis for a chronology, suggesting that Romans was written from Greece (Acts 20.2) around 56 or 57 as Paul was preparing to go to Jerusalem (Rom. 15.25) with the money he had collected for the saints, that is, poor believers (cf. Gal. 2.10; 1 Cor. 16.1-4; 2 Cor. 8–9).

There were many Gentiles in Rome and it is intelligible that Paul, who considered himself (1.1, 9-15) (and was acknowledged by others, Gal. 2.9) an apostle to the Gentiles, should want to visit the capital and proclaim the gospel there, as he says at 1.10-15. Near the end of his epistle (15.22-24) he is more specific about his plans for a Western mission to Spain, helped on his way by Roman believers. A suspicious reader may wonder whether Paul's eye was more on Rome than the Costa Brava, but there is no doubting Paul's ambitions and either way he would naturally write to believers in Rome and prepare for his visit. His missionary practice of exempting Gentile converts from observing the law of Moses was highly controversial (see Galatians). It would therefore be sensible for him to prepare for his visit with a letter explaining his position and seeking to persuade them he was right. That would not be easy and could well backfire. It would be more tactful to give a positive account of his own position, or of what God was doing among the Gentiles, than to dispute directly the central convictions of some of the believers in Rome. It would be natural to give them some idea of what he preached but to allow this account of his understanding of the gospel to address indirectly the disputed question of whether Gentile converts should observe the Torah.

It is thus possible to explain in terms of his projected visit and future mission plans why Paul wrote what is evidently his most systematic epistle, to believers in a major city that he had not yet visited. It would still be necessary to explore how far this exposition was designed to gain support or allay suspicions, and whether that aim had affected the presentation, but this general aim attributed to Paul is plausible. It also corresponds fairly well to the way Romans has usually been read by protestant theologians. Ever since Melanchthon wrote his *Loci Communes* (doctrinal topics) in 1521, following the general structure of Romans, the epistle has been treated as a handbook of Christian doctrine. It is not quite that, but if we can imagine Paul summing up his missionary theology and experience, then both its dominant position among the apostle's letters and the way it has been used in much systematic theology can be defended. The completion of his mission in the East and his plans to turn West (15.16-24) provide a credible setting for this sort of theological exposition.

If, as seems likely, Paul's Western mission did not materialize, on account of his arrest in Jerusalem (Acts 21) and arrival in Rome as a prisoner, this epistle then stands as Paul's 'testament', and the later church was right to give it pride of place when it honoured the apostle in its canon.

Trouble in Rome?

On the view sketched above, the discussion of disagreements over food in ch. 14 can be seen as a generalization based on experience gained elsewhere (1 Cor. 8), just as Romans 12 seems briefly to echo 1 Corinthians 12–14 on ministries and love. But letters are usually shaped by the situation they address and if the long list of contacts in ch. 16 was an original part of the epistle it is probable that Paul was well-informed about the situation in Rome. Given his strong sense of apostolic responsibility, and despite his cautious tone at 1.8, 12 and 15.14 it is equally possible that Paul wrote with an eye to the actual situation existing among the believers in Rome. The emphasis upon 'all', Jews and Gentiles, in the first three chapters may be significant here, and possibly the absence of the word 'church' in the address. Paul was writing to them all and perhaps trying to bring different groups together into a united church (15.5-7).

It is hard to doubt that there were both Jewish and Gentile Christians in Rome in the 50s. Some Jews had been expelled from Rome by Claudius, probably in 41 or possibly 49 CE, and very likely as a result of disturbances in a synagogue over

Jewish-Christian preaching. (The Roman historian
Suetonius writes of a tumult connected with 'Chrestus'.)
They were allowed back under Nero, who became emperor in
54. Prisca and Aquila were among those expelled (Acts 18.2).
Unless Romans 16 was written to Ephesus, as some have
suggested, they had apparently returned by the time Paul
was writing (16.3). It seems likely that the recently returned
Jewish Christians and the Gentile Christians belonged in
different house-churches with little contact, and it is not
hard to believe that one of Paul's purposes in writing was to
bring about some rapprochement between them.

Romans 14 gives specific advice for handling disputes over
food and festival observance. Verses 17 and 21 mention drink
(wine) and v. 20 indicates that purity rules were at issue.
15.8-9 shows that Paul's concern is over the relationship of
Jews and Gentiles. Food was a flashpoint in relations
between Jewish and Gentile Christians, as we know from
Antioch (Gal. 2.11-14) and Corinth. The problem was not
vegetarianism (as it seems to a modern reader) and is
unlikely to have been pork chops (unclean food). It was probably Jewish sensitivity about idolatry. Drinking wine or
eating meat that had been offered to an idol was intolerable
and the possibility of this would make eating with Gentiles
(or even sharing the eucharist?) dangerous. Better stick to
vegetables (14.2), and worship separately (cf. 15.6-7).

This also is a plausible line of interpretation for chs.
14–15.13, and it is possible to see how chs. 1–13 might
provide support or underpinning for such an ecumenical aim.
Gentiles are told to respect Jewish priority (11.13) and much
of the argument could be designed to persuade Jewish
Christians to accept the law-free Gentile mission. The fit is
not tight—the emphasis is far more on persuading Jewish
Christians—but in such situations it is always the conserva-
tives who need to be persuaded of the legitimacy of a new
development.

It is not necessary to choose between these two types of
historical explanation, one rooted in Paul's plans and situation and the other in that of his hearers. They are compatible, even if we decide to emphasize one more than the other.
They also overlap. If Paul were responding to Roman

criticisms of his gospel and mission (contrary to Acts 28.22) that would correspond both to his advance plans and to the situation in Rome (Acts 28.22 is a doubtful witness to the latter). All suggestions are partly circular, being based on what the epistle is thought to say, and then that being used to interpret the text. We might talk of an 'implied situation' to remind ourselves that our suggestions are hypothetical and provisional, to be tested by what sense they make of the whole epistle and whatever external information is also available.

Instruction or Persuasion?

One possible reservation about reconstructions of Paul's aims which place the emphasis on his wanting to remedy the situation in Rome is the caution and indirectness of his approach. We can explain his silence about the actual situation in Rome as tact (1.12; 15.14). Even his praise can be read as courtesy. But the indirectness of his argument may be a sign of something else, and the 'Roman situation' explanation does not do full justice to the indications that Paul is having to defend his own position (3.8; perhaps 9.1; 10.1). Even if we give priority to the supposed situation in Rome, as may now do, this may not be a sufficient explanation. The sinister tone of 15.30-32 coupled with our partial knowledge (from Acts 21) of the outcome suggests that the epistle needs to be related to Paul's immediate concerns as well as his plans.

The projected visit to Rome explains the positive content of the epistle and even the elements of personal self-defence, but does not quite do justice to the *argumentative* current in the epistle. In ch. 1 it sounds as though it will be mainly exposition, but ch. 2 and the beginning of ch. 3 are more argumentative, and even the exposition of 3.19-26 leads into some diatribe followed by scriptural argument. Chapters 5–8 look like exposition, but contain an implicit argument that Christian experience is Spirit based (cf. Gal. 3.1-5) and chs. 9–10 are again dominated by scriptural argument. Theories about Paul's aims need to explain why the epistle contains theological argument as well as theological exposition and moral exhortation.

Another feature of the letter that makes it different from a systematic exposition is the way Paul's concern with the law keeps cropping up outside the major treatment in ch. 7, and in ways that say more than the context requires (i.e. at 2.12-27; 3.19-31; 4.13-16; 5.13, 20; 6.14-15; 8.2-4; 9.31; 10.4-5; 13.8-10). This does not look like Paul's 'doctrine of the law' section of a systematic exposition. It might reflect the personal problem of one who has changed his religious position and rejected what was once his pride and joy (cf. Phil. 3.7), but it might be something more subtle and more serious. The curious combination of negative and positive things said about the law is better explained as an argument similar to Galatians being tempered by an attempt to be conciliatory. Paul acknowledges the role of the law in salvation history, its positive witness, and the validity of its moral content, but argues from Scripture and experience that righteousness is through faith, not works of the law. The central claim of Galatians is repeated, but everything possible said about the place of Israel and the law in God's plan, and its necessary witness and valid moral content for the present. Not that this finally explains why God gave a law which would ultimately prove inadequate, but God is after all inscrutable (11.33-36).

In Galatians this argument is directed at Paul's Gentile converts who are wanting to observe the Torah, as the Judaizers insist. In Rome there is no sign of any such argument, but it seems likely that the issue of the law is equally central to both. It might have surfaced in a practical way over table-fellowship and shared worship, but it posed questions which went to the heart of Christian identity and what forms Christian mission should take among Jews and Gentiles. Romans is less systematic than Melanchthon's *Loci* but it is equally theological. It grapples with the question of what Christianity *is*, even if that question was occasioned by a practical problem. Paul's highly contentious answer is here more than half-concealed behind a celebration of what God is now doing among Gentiles no less than Jews. The promised gospel (1.2), the revelation of God's righteousness (1.17; 3.21) in the coming of messiah, that is, the sending of his Son (8.3), was not a matter of dispute between Paul and his addressees, neither was faith (1.17) nor the sacrificial death of Christ (3.25; 8.3, 32), his resurrection (1.4; 4.25; 10.9), lordship, the Spirit (1.4) and its gifts (12.6-8), baptism (6.3-5), membership of the people of God (1.7, 9-11), morality (*passim*) and the hope of future salvation (13.11). The apostle to the Gentiles could therefore wrap up his theological arguments in a great flannel of uncontroversial theological exposition and doxology—praise and thanksgiving, prayer and passion—all appropriate to a letter of self-introduction prior to a planned first visit.

No doubt there were Jewish and perhaps Gentile Christians who shared the Galatian Judaizers' point of view. It was the common sense position for Jewish Christians and even for Gentiles attracted to the synagogue. Jesus had not revoked the law of Moses or the covenant within which it was the gift of God. Others in Rome, Jews like Prisca and Aquila as well as Gentiles, shared Paul's more radical view. The absence of polemic in this epistle corresponds to Paul's being positive about the law (cf. 7.7-25) and holding dislocated human nature (flesh) rather than the law itself (8.3) responsible for the failure of the law to set people free in a right relationship to God. It suggests that he is trying partly to persuade *Jewish* Christians, even though he is at least at times explicitly addressing *Gentile* believers and emphasizing his apostolate to the Gentiles (1.13-15; 11.13; 15.15-29). The substance of the argument from Scripture and experience addressed to Judaizing Gentiles in Galatia is in Paul's opinion true for everyone and therefore equally applicable to Jewish Christians in Rome and anywhere else, including Jerusalem: that following God's end-time intervention by the sending of his Son (Rom. 8.3; Gal. 4.4) a right relationship is found *this* way (by faith and receiving the Spirit) not *that* way—through observance of the Jewish religious system (Gal. 2.16; Rom. 3.21). The moral intention of the law is now fulfilled by those who walk according to the Spirit (Rom. 8.4, cf. Gal. 5).

An Eye to Jerusalem

One important detail to be given due weight in our account of Paul's plans is what he says about his more immediate task of going to Jerusalem with the collection (15.25). We would expect this to have been more on his mind than medium-term plans to visit Spain—or even Rome—and that is confirmed by ch. 15. His proposed Roman visit receives due emphasis. It is his excuse for writing, certainly one of his reasons. There is no doubt that Paul sees his work in the East as complete, however extraordinary that appears to us. His perspective was shortened by his expectation of the parousia (13.11, cf. 1 Thess. 4–5; 1 Cor. 15; Phil. 4.5). But now he is going to Jerusalem to minister to the saints (15.25). He attaches great importance to this and it may help explain why he wrote to Rome.

He begs for their prayers (15.30), that he might be rescued from those in Judaea who do not believe, and that his offering might be acceptable to the saints (v. 31). This would be an indication that his law-free Gentile mission was accepted, as it was at least provisionally at the so-called council of Jerusalem (Gal. 2.1-10; Acts 15).

Despite Acts 21 we do not know exactly what happened, or whether the money (which Acts 21 does not mention, but cf. 24.17) was accepted. Paul may have seen it as the fulfilment of prophecy—the Gentiles bringing their gifts to Zion (Isa.60). Later Jewish–Christian hostility to his memory makes it doubtful whether some of the Jerusalem leadership ever accepted the gift or Paul's mission, but in the martyrdom of James in 62 CE and the fall of Jerusalem in 70 CE history overtook that now lost confrontation.

Paul's request for the Romans' prayers that the money be accepted might surprise those familiar with religious organizations. It suggests that the outlook was at best uncertain. Perhaps he wrote this epistle wanting his position 'on the record' at an important centre, in case the argument in Jerusalem went against him, as it had in Antioch a few years before. Perhaps he was aiming to win Jewish Christian support for his position in the hope that they might exercise some influence on the Jerusalem church. We know that the

Jewish community in Rome maintained close contacts with Jerusalem. Or perhaps the arguments he would marshall in Jerusalem were already shaping his thoughts. Any of these variations on an explanation that places most weight on Paul's imminent journey to Jerusalem is compatible with his conciliatory attitude to the law. The body of the epistle seems directed at Jewish Christians, even though Paul is (at least some of the time) addressing Gentile converts.

The Direction of the Argument

Another possibility is that Paul is arguing with the Jewish Christian he knows best, namely himself. It is surely correct that Paul would need to explain to himself why God was now offering salvation to the Gentiles by another route. It had taken a resurrection appearance to convert him, so he cannot have been surprised that Israel as a whole was not convinced. The puzzle was not so much Israel's unbelief as God's apparent change of plan. Why did God provide in the Mosaic covenant with Israel a way of salvation that was ultimately to prove inadequate? Scriptural exploration of this must have been a theological necessity for Paul himself, even if it ran into the sand of God's inscrutability.

That aspect of the problem is perhaps visible when Paul offers an explanation of the law's purpose, but it does not fit the epistle as a whole. Here Paul is surely arguing his case and trying to persuade Jewish Christians of his conviction that God is calling Jews and Gentiles alike into a relationship based on faith in Christ, not observance of Torah. But the argument is far less direct than in Galatians. Paul is seeking to reassure Jewish Christians by insisting on morality and protesting his loyalty to Israel. He is as positive as he can be about the law without yielding an inch on his central conviction which denies it a constitutive role in the present revelation of God's righteousness, allowing it only to bear witness to this and to declare the moral content of God's holy will.

It seems that the position of the law in God's saving activity rather than 'justification by faith' or 'the people of God' is Paul's underlying concern throughout this theological argument. Then why is it not directly mentioned in the state-

ment of his theme at 1.16-17? The emphatic inclusion there
of Jews as also being brought to salvation by faith does imply
a denial that they are put right with God through Torah
observance, but that negation about the law does not become
explicit until 3.20. It seems we have to distinguish in this
epistle between Paul's main concern and his explicit theme.

It has already emerged that in Romans, as in Galatians, a
case is being argued, not a system being constructed. That
seems likely despite the lack of polemic, the invisibility of
any opponents, and the strong element of exposition and
doxology in this epistle. All these differences have been
explained, and the similarity of aim is confirmed by the
similar way that Scripture is used in Romans 4 and
Galatians 3–4. The texts quoted contribute to an argument,
rather than proof-texting a doctrinal proposition. The
element of doctrinal statement found here is not the goal to
which the texts point but itself part of an unstated argument
that Gentiles need not observe Torah and be circumcised.
Romans contains nothing so direct as Gal. 2.21 or 5.2, but
Paul uses the same central scriptural argument linking
righteousness with faith, and the practical aim of his
argument is presumably the same.

The similarities to Galatians may provide the best clue to
what is going on below the surface in Romans. How these
are weighed, and how far the differences between the two
epistles are stressed, explains some of the variety of interpretations of Romans. The comparison therefore demands
attention.

The central claim that a right relationship to God is based
on faith (Jesus Christ faith), not Torah observance, is the
same in Galatians and Romans. Some of the same Old
Testament texts are used to argue it from Scripture,
including the two which associated 'right' language with
faith or believing (Gen. 15.6; Hab. 2.4). The Gal. 3.1-5 argument from the nature of Christian experience as life in the
Spirit may also have its counterpart in Romans 5–8, and the
Spirit basis for Christian behaviour (Gal. 5) is similar to
Romans 8. Baptism is said to constitute an intimate relationship with the crucified and risen Christ at Gal. 3.27 as in
Rom. 6.3-5.

These correspondences are enough to suggest a similar underlying argument, expanded in Romans by discussions of the human plight (1.18–3.19; 5.12–7.24) which exonerate the law from blame, and consideration of the position of Israel (9–11) which was less relevant to the situation in Galatia, and the inclusion of more Christian moral content and theory. It is natural to ask why Paul should have repeated and refined his earlier arguments. Perhaps he had come to regard them the most penetrating way of expounding his understanding of the gospel, as Marcion (imperfectly) and Luther (more perfectly) were to think. They would then fit the aim of theological exposition. But they gain their edge from what they deny, and that denial must have been intended to defend the legitimacy of Paul's law-free Gentile mission. It is likely that there were Jewish Christians in Rome whom he needed to persuade of this. The arguments used in Galatians were the best he had and as appropriate to Jewish Christians in Rome and shortly in Jerusalem, as to Judaizing Gentiles (and over their shoulder to Judaizers) in Galatia.

The near absence of Paul's scriptural 'right' language elsewhere, except where Judaizers are perhaps being warned against in Philippians 3, suggests that this was part of a specific scriptural argument making a particular case rather than the way Paul normally expressed himself in articulating the gospel. It almost disappears from Romans 6–8 where Paul is no longer arguing from Scripture, as well as from the other epistles where again the use of Scripture is rarer. That conclusion need not devalue this particular part of Paul's language which has been found to have a wider applicability than he probably intended. Its power derives from its sharp antithetical formulation. When something is excluded or denied, the positive statement sometimes shines through more clearly. The antithesis remains sharp even without the polemical tone of Galatians.

The suggestion being pursued here is that the combination of similarities to and differences from Galatians, where Paul's aims are relatively clear, throws light on his aims in Romans which are unclear. Again Paul needs to persuade his hearers that Gentile converts do not have to observe the

Torah and be circumcised. But he also needs to reassure his Roman hearers that rumours about his disregard for morality (3.8) and disloyalty to Israel (3.1) are unfounded. That could in part explain the heavily moralistic section 1.18–3.20 and the section on Israel in chs. 9–11.

Both these major sections can also be related to the situation in Rome. The strong Jewish community was not without problems of its own, noted by Josephus (*Ant.* 18.81-84), and these might possibly be alluded to at 2.19-24. The warnings of ch. 11 would fit a situation in which Gentile converts were now outnumbering Jewish Christians. More important, these sections contribute to the main argument that a right relationship to God depends on 'faith' not on 'works of law'. Chapters 9-11 do so directly in 9.30–10.21, chs. 1–3 do so indirectly by showing that all, Jews and Gentiles, are in the same predicament, thus reinforcing the argument that *all* are put right (and so will be saved) in the same way too. Paul introduces this main argument cautiously, under cover of matters that were not contentious among Jewish Christians. In view of his audience that was prudent.

Some Roman believers might have asked what business Paul had writing to them at all. His own view was clear. He was apostle to the Gentiles, called by God (1.1) (a call incidentally acknowledged in Jerusalem, Gal. 2.9), and there were Gentiles in Rome. It is these he addresses directly at 11.13. But he directs his epistle to *all* believers in Rome (1.7). He urges them to accept one another (15.7) and the names greeted in ch. 16 include both Jews and Gentiles. His argument is not now directed to Gentiles in danger of Judaizing, but its substance is the same: that Gentiles do not have to do the works of the law (notably male circumcision, food laws, and sabbath observance) in order to fulfil God's will contained in the law and summed up in the love command.

He could make this argument direct when writing to churches he had founded, and reasserting his apostolic authority. Rome was different. He had no standing beyond his apostolic commission and can only proclaim his message in positive terms. The negative implication is subdued, often obtruded through ambiguous formulations (3.27; 8.2; 9.31; 10.4) but always present and sometimes explicit (3.20a; 7.6;

8.3)—though in each of those cases the negative is at once qualified by positive statements about the role, nature or content of the Torah. The most clearly negative message conveyed about the law is conveyed not by anything said directly but by grouping it with sin and death (5.12–7.6), in contrast to the Spirit and life (7.6; 8). Even here the worst that is said about it is that believers are freed from it.

The positive rubric under which Paul proclaims his gospel in Romans (and only in Romans) is God's righteousness. Righteousness is a strong biblical word, central to the religious vocabulary of Judaism, capable of bearing the great weight Paul places on it in Romans. The full force of this scriptural term will become clearer in our next chapter, but even our preliminary reading rang bells from the Old Testament, especially the Psalter's celebration of God's righteousness being revealed in the presence of the nations or Gentiles. Paul's quotations and allusions to the Psalter enable the noun to evoke his Gentile mission, and to carry strong connotations of salvation. It also ties up with the cognate verb which Paul found in a negative formulation at Ps. 143 (LXX 142).2 and alluded to at Gal. 2.16 and Rom. 3.20.

Paul can use the noun to refer to God's righteousness (saving action and holy nature) and to humans' right relationship to God and their right behaviour. He can use the adjective theologically to describe the right relationship with God, or ethically; these are not separated in his Jewish thought. He can use the verb with more or less of a forensic flavour, but always in a positive sense. It speaks of vindication, that is, salvation, not just deserts in Paul's usage. The flexibility of this terminology allows the apostle to articulate his gospel and celebrate what God is now doing among the Gentiles, while making room for his sub-text about how God is now bringing all to salvation, and where this is not to be found (9.31).

Relationship or Membership?

This account of Paul's aims has placed the emphasis upon the 'soteriological' or salvation aspect of Paul's 'right' language, corresponding to the use of 'right' words in the

Psalter and 2 Isaiah (e.g. Isa. 45.21). We have also noted the difference between the time references of Paul's words about *right* and his word *salvation*. The former normally refer to the past or present (the occasional future tenses, 2.13; 3.20, 30, probably have a logical rather than a temporal force in Paul's mind) whereas Paul's *salvation* language (unlike Eph. 2.5, 8) has a mainly future aspect (see above, p. 26). This past and present time reference of 'right' language, and the view of some that the phrase 'works of the law' in Romans as in Galatians refers primarily to circumcision, the rite of entry into the people of God through the Mosaic covenant, suggest that Paul's concerns are more 'ecclesiological' than our description has implied. Was Paul perhaps more concerned with the conditions of entry into the new covenant community than with the character of a new relationship with God?

The alternative has to be resisted. For a Jew like Paul relationship with God is through being a member of the covenant people of God. Paul did not give up that corporate dimension when he redefined the people of God in the light of the new covenant (1 Cor. 11.25; 2 Cor. 3.6, cf. Rom. 7.6), that is, what God was now doing in the gospel—creating a new community of Jews and Gentiles in Christ and bringing 'all' to salvation. Even though 'faith' is an individual responsibility and no one can have it for you, Paul was not a religious individualist. His life was spent building up communities and it was in these communities that Christ faith existed. On the other hand Paul rarely speaks about being a Christian ('in Christ', having faith) in terms of membership of these communities. He speaks of it in terms of relationship with Christ and sees believers' relationships to one another as grounded in that and deriving from that. Faith is entirely determined by its object, namely Christ, that is, God as known in the gospel concerning his Son. Paul's 'right' language is normally fused with faith (2.13 and 6.7 are easily explained exceptions). Granted the weight 'faith' (in Christ) has in Paul, it is questionable to reduce his 'right' language to talk about entrance requirements, and so shift the focus from christology to ecclesiology, even though Paul does have this practical issue in mind. His language is richer and his thought deeper and directed towards God. His evident concern with some fragile religious institutions should not obscure the force of his biblical language.

Recent emphases on the community aspect of Paul's 'right' language are partly a reaction against Protestant individualism, partly a new respect for Paul's positive attitude in Romans to his kinsfolk Israel, partly a new sense of the historical and social context of his letters, and partly Bonhoeffer's secular Christian feeling that Luther's question about finding a gracious God has been widely replaced by the search for a gracious neighbour—where to find true community. None of these valid insights need obscure the primacy of christology in Paul's theology in general or the theocentric character of Romans in particular. Paul's gospel establishes humans' relationship to God based on faith. That involves membership of an institution and interpersonal relationships and ministries within the church, but these derive from the Spirit given in baptism following the 'hearing of faith'.

Paul's thinking about the human relationship with God must have been so shaped by God's covenant with Israel that we might expect his new Christian thinking to follow a similar pattern. The new covenant established by the death and resurrection of Jesus, God's eschatological act inaugurating the new age, is indeed central and unfolds in his account of the believer's relationship to Christ (faith, 'in Christ'). But Paul does not much articulate life in Christ (life in the Spirit) in terms of membership of the new community, the enlarged people of God, the historic church. Considering that his entire apostolic activity consisted in establishing and guiding churches it is surprising how little he theorizes about ' the Church'. Interpreters' judgments about the nuances of Paul's theology must depend upon an intimate knowledge of all his writings. That judgment assumes that the highly ecclesiological epistle to the Ephesians was not written by Paul.

There is room for disagreement about the nuances of Paul's theology and about how much weight to give to each of Paul's possible aims in writing Romans. We do not have enough information to be dogmatic about historical questions. It will therefore be wise to bear all reasonable possibilities in mind as we continue to read the epistle, since to exclude any might exclude a perspective relevant for understanding the text. Some suggestions, however, can be set aside and others accepted as truisms which do not affect how we read Romans.

Paul doubtless aimed to communicate the Christian message (as he understood it) in every letter he wrote. To list that as an aim does not throw much light until the situation in which he was writing is elucidated. The kind of communication he wrote is also relevant here. Romans contains different literary styles, from argument to doxology, but in the foreground is an exposition and celebration of what God is now doing, and behind that a sharp argument about how God is doing it and how not, with an implication for present missionary policy.

Paul was a thinker, and agonized about the implications of his present beliefs about what God was now doing among the Gentiles as well as Jews in the sending of his Son. But any suggestion that in Romans Paul is simply thinking aloud or rehearsing his future Jerusalem speech can be discounted. He was writing to a specific audience and suggestions about his purposes must be related to that, even if in fact (as is credible) Paul planned to argue along similar lines in Jerusalem. The main three emphases we have singled out can be combined in different ways, e.g. to suggest that Paul's main concern was to answer Roman objections to his theology and missionary practice. They are all compatible with each other and suggested by the text itself and by what else we know about Paul and Christianity in Rome at that time. They will guide our ongoing reading and rereading Romans. Which was the most important reason for Paul writing (his plan to visit Rome and Spain; the situation in Rome; or his impending visit to Jerusalem) is unclear, but his most immediate concern was surely the third.

We can make no claim to detailed knowledge of Paul's mind, but can only select what seems to throw most light on the text itself. The difficulties in making historical inferences on the basis of this epistle can best be explained on the supposition that Paul was playing a delicate hand, half concealing his main concern, which was highly controversial (especially among Jewish Christians), behind his main theme of God's present activity which (among believers) was not. The next move is to see whether the hypothesis is confirmed by its success in making the text more intelligible. It would therefore make sense at this point either to reread Chapter 2, or proceed to a closer look at some particular parts of the epistle in our next chapter. Further details on *The Reasons for Romans* can be found in a book with that title by A.J.M. Wedderburn (1991) and a collection of essays on *The Romans Debate* (ed. K.P. Donfried, rev. edn 1991).

4

SCRIPTURE AND
TRADITION IN ROMANS

IN OUR INITIAL READINGS of the epistle and discussion of Paul's possible aims in writing, two related features emerged: some similarities with Galatians (along with some differences), and Paul's unusually heavy dependence on his Scripture, the Greek Old Testament or Septuagint (LXX). Galatians uses some of the same texts, suggesting a similar underlying scriptural argument even though the explicit theme and main focus of Romans is different. That provisional suggestion will now be tested and confirmed by a closer look at Paul's use of his Bible in Romans, and its relation to his thematic statement at 1.16-17.

Scripture is usually a most important part of any religious believer's tradition. It provides a language of prayer and praise as well as doctrine and argument. But for Paul and other followers of Jesus, their Scriptures spoke at best indirectly about what was central to their faith and experience. They were therefore also dependent on more recent traditions which spoke of Jesus the messiah, his death and resurrection (see 1 Cor. 15.3-5). Writing to believers in a city he had not yet visited and where perhaps he was not universally loved or trusted, it would be natural for Paul to quote or echo both Scripture and liturgical formulations familiar to his hearers in order to assure them they all shared a common faith (see p. 125).

Biblical allusions are profuse in Romans 1–11, but the distribution of actual quotations throughout the epistle is quite uneven. They are almost absent in ch. 1 which contains only the vital Hab. 2.4 in v. 17. The allusions to the Psalter noted above (p. 20) in vv. 16-17 are (in our judgment) equally important, but less obvious and often missed by commentators. Biblical quotations are surprisingly rare in chs. 2, and 5–8; chs. 12–14 contain only a few and 15.22 to the end (naturally enough) none at all. These infrequencies underline the density of scriptural reference elsewhere.

Statistics are misleading because Paul sometimes piles up quotations without advancing the argument much. The seven or so confirmatory quotations at 3.10-18 say much less than the five in ch. 4 which constitute an elaborate argument. Romans 9–11 contains several important scriptural arguments, whereas the Psalm quoted at 8.36, like the quotation of Proverbs at 12.20, contributes little to the argument. These function rhetorically in other ways.

It is impossible to discuss here all 54 (or so) biblical quotations in Romans, much less all Paul's biblical allusions, and unnecessary to repeat the minute analyses of some specialist monographs. A broad brush will be enough to illuminate the epistle as a whole.

Chapter 15

The beginning and end of a composition are often revealing, and ch. 15 has already told us much about Paul's plans and possible reasons for writing. The biblical quotations in that chapter may also prove instructive. The passion Psalm (69.9) quoted in v. 3 was widely used in early Christian preaching and has no special significance here. The quotation from the Song of the Suffering Servant (Isa. 52.15) which rounds off the paragraph in v. 21 again merely confirms the specific point about not building on others' foundations. But the string of quotations in vv. 9-12 is striking. All four celebrate God's activity among the Gentiles and are referred by their context to the Gentile mission which takes place alongside God's confirmation of his promises to the fathers (v. 8).

The references to the promises (v. 8) and to the God of hope at the end of the paragraph (v. 13) echo earlier chapters. In the first detailed scriptural argument (ch.4) the promise to

Abraham is pitted against the law of Moses in order to include *Gentiles* among the seed of Abraham (Gen. 17.5; 15.5) And Abraham's hope is celebrated and seen as an aspect of his faith. Form and content are different in 15.9-12. Two of the four quotations are from the Psalter (18.49; 117.1) one from Deut. 32.43, and one from Isa. 11.10. But the word that links them all is *Gentiles* and the thought that connects them is Paul's presence among the Gentiles and his celebration of what God is doing to bring them also into a right relationship.

This cluster of quotations supports a statement about God's activity among both Jews and Gentiles which is attached to Paul's plea that believers in Rome accept one another as Christ accepted them. The promises to the fathers have been discussed in chs. 4 and 9–11; here it is the Gentile mission that is celebrated and perhaps implicitly defended. Calling the Jewish people 'the circumcision' here in v. 8 implies a reference to the Gentiles as uncircumcision (cf. 3.30; 4.9-12) and possibly therefore to Gentile converts as free from the requirement of circumcision. Certainly it is his own law-free Gentile mission that Paul has in mind in this context (15.15-21).

In 15.9-12 Paul applies to his own generation the language of Scripture (especially the Psalter) about the nations or Gentiles (*ethne*). This takes us back to the proposal made (p. 20) about the psalm references hovering behind Rom. 1.16-17, and so defining the theme of the whole epistle. The allusions are not obvious, but they may explain his new key term 'the righteousness of God'. The phrase does not occur in earlier epistles except at 2 Cor. 5.21 which is different, describing not the divine action but the resulting Christian condition.

The Psalms have much to say about God's righteousness as well as human righteousness, and most of that is concerned with salvation. Like Isa. 51.4-8, Ps. 85 (LXX 84) speaks three times each of 'righteousness' and 'salvation' and contains several other elements of Romans' theological vocabulary (God's wrath, anger, kindness, truth, mercy, peace). Ps. 94 (LXX 93).14 anticipates the theme of Romans 9–11: 'For the Lord will not forsake his people' (*aposetai*, cf. Rom. 11.1:

aposato), and relates it to the keyword righteousness: 'he will not abandon his heritage until righteousness return unto judgment'.

Most of the theological vocabulary of Romans can be found in the Greek Psalter, but what Paul is primarily interested in is best expressed in Psalm 96 (LXX 95) with its new song of good news (*euaggelizomai*) of salvation (v. 2) to be sung by all the earth (v. 1), and the instruction to tell of God's glory among the nations or Gentiles (v. 3), to say there that the Lord has begun to rule (v. 10 inceptive aorist), and that he is coming (v. 13) and that this final judgment will (be good, because it will) involve God's righteousness and truth (cf. v. 13). The heavens have begun (inceptive aorist) to declare this righteousness (of God) and all the peoples to see his glory (LXX Ps. 96.6). The Lord made known (or has begun to make known) his salvation; in the face of the Gentiles he has begun to reveal his (saving) righteousness (LXX Ps. 97.2).

The Psalmist's own interest is plain in the next verse. God remembered his mercy to Jacob, and his truth to the house of Israel. 'All the ends of the earth' are more spectators than beneficiaries of God's salvation for Israel, but they too can celebrate the Good Thing that they have witnessed—God's righteousness, mercy and truth. Paul reads all this in the light of his experience of what God is now doing not only among the Gentiles and in their presence, but for them.

Chapter 4

The main frame of the epistle, containing scriptural echoes at 1.16 and quotations at 15.9-12, proclaims and celebrates what God is now doing among the Gentiles. Inside this frame and introduced as early as 1.17, Paul uses Scripture (as in Gal. 3) in a more technical way to argue his controversial case that what God is now doing is based on faith, not Torah observance. The positive statement is introduced with the quotation from Hab. 2.4 at 1.17 (cf. Gal. 3.11) but the negative, based on Ps. 143.2 and introduced at the outset in Gal. 2.16, is prepared for more cautiously by Romans 2 before surfacing at 3.20. The scriptural argument in ch.4 is based on Gen. 15.6 (cf. Gal. 3.6). (This verse is quoted in vv. 3 and 9 and echoed in vv. 4-5, 10-13, 18-24.) Like Hab. 2.4 (and nowhere else in the Septuagint) it bases humans' right relationship with God on faith.

Unlike Galatians 3, Romans 4 enriches the argument with a quotation from the Psalter (see p. 33). Unusually for Paul, this interprets right relationship with God, based on faith, in terms of forgiveness. That suggestion was taken up by Luther in his quest for a gracious God, making justification interpreted as forgiveness the heart of the gospel. Paul's point was simply to reinforce his denial that Torah observance was necessary. He takes David's beatitude to confirm his own 'apart from works' (v. 6). The works that are said to be superfluous for coming into a right relationship with God through faith are probably the ritual system (by which some sins were dealt with in Judaism). It is circumcision, not morality as such, that Paul has in mind. The criticism of Paul in Jas 2.14-26 is based on a misunderstanding of Romans.

Paul's negative (not by Torah observance) is not made fully explicit in this chapter until vv. 13-14 which use the actual word *law*. Here he casts the law into a shadow by discussing the promise which was made to Abraham through righteousness based on faith, not through Torah observance.

Introducing the contentious negative (about the law) through an uncontroversial positive affirmation (here the promise) is a tactic we observed in ch. 2. The promise is particularly appropriate to Paul's argument because promises in general require faith (trust) and need bear no relation to law (cf. vv. 14 and 16). Paul could scarcely have argued in this way had he thought (as some think) mainly in terms of the 'covenant' (cf. 9.4), since God's covenant with Israel does connect God's promise with keeping the law. His concern here is to insist that the content of the promise, that Abraham or his seed should inherit the world, concerns Gentiles as well as Jews (v. 17, quoting Gen. 17.5). He then goes on to associate Abraham's faith with Christian faith, implicitly in vv. 17b-19 by talk of God giving life to the dead and creating new life from dead bodies, and explicitly in vv. 24-25 by references to Jesus' resurrection.

The argument is less complicated than Galatians 3, and

more persuasive. It focuses more clearly on the figure of Abraham and makes two simple points about him: (1) that his right relationship with God was based on his faith response to God's initiative, not on 'works' (v. 2), that is, the God-given rituals which signify Jewish identity; and (2) that he is the father of all believers, circumcised and uncircumcised.

The first argument is reinforced by an appeal to David, whose Psalms dominate the intertextuality of Romans. By speaking of the person who is righted 'without works' (v. 6, cf. 3.20), David becomes a witness to righteousness being by faith, not by Torah observance.

The part of the law with which Paul is in practice most concerned surfaces in v. 9 (as at 2.25) with the mention of circumcision. Plugging a hole in the argument of Galatians this is now assessed in v. 11 as merely a seal of the real thing, which is right relationship with God, based on faith. What that has led to, in God's plan, is the inclusion of uncircumcised Gentiles.

The argument here is not complicated by reflection on the mechanics of atonement as in Galatians 3. Paul has said quite enough about that at 3.24-26, and can therefore make his scriptural argument simpler than in Galatians. Even so, he cannot resist complicating it in v. 15 by reflecting briefly on the *purpose of the law*, as at 3.20b and 5.20. His underlying concern with the law keeps interrupting the positive argument about salvation and faith. More importantly, the chapter's focus on Abraham, the man of faith, allows Paul to link his concern with the inclusion of uncircumcised Gentiles to the promised event of new life out of death which achieves this. The fertility of old Abraham and Sarah is a kind of resurrection, analogous to the resurrection which followed the death of Christ. Scripture refers to the present time (v. 24, cf. 15.4; 1 Cor. 9.10).

5.12-21

That typological use of Scripture, developed in Rom. 5.12-21, is quite different from the argument based on scriptural quotation in ch. 4. Here what God has achieved in Christ is described by means of a contrast with the equally far-reaching event of Adam's transgression. Genesis 2-3 is not quoted; the story is presupposed. Again the presentation is slightly distorted by the intrusion of Paul's preoccupation with the position of the Jewish law (vv. 13, 21), but the general picture is clear enough. The universal dimensions of the liberation achieved by Christ's obedience are expressed by contrasting it with Adam's disobedience. Naturally the divine act (grace) outweighs human sin, and a rhetorical insistence on this (grace abounding) provides a cue for Paul to answer a serious objection to his theology and missionary practice of waiving the law: why not go on sinning so that grace may abound?

Paul's answer does not involve Scripture so must be deferred to the next chapter, but his claim that believers are freed from sin (ch. 6) and also from the law (7.1-6) is built on the mythological picture introduced here. His spatial metaphor of entire realms being ruled by sin and death (or by the alternative) depends on the Genesis myth. This is also echoed at 7.11 even though it is the tenth commandment that is quoted (7.7) and the law that is being discussed. All this pervasive presence of Scripture, even where it is scarcely quoted, will prompt further reflection, but first the most text-intensive part of the epistle summarized in pp. 49-56 calls for some additional comment.

Chapters 9-11

Israel's (partial) unbelief was mentioned at 3.3. God's faithfulness and truth were asserted and confirmed with a quotation from Psalm 51. In any legal contest between God and humanity God must triumph. That reference to the 'justification of God' bears almost no relation to Paul's account of believers being righted or 'justified by faith' (5.1). Luther's glorious lecture on this section (English pp. 66-72) thus seems to confuse the issue, but at a deeper level Luther understood Paul better than most modern historians and exegetes because he understood something of how talk of God finally defies rational analysis.

Paul's collection of scriptural and other arguments in Romans 9–11 presupposes the biblical pattern of a world and history subject to the plan of God who is unquestionably good but not answerable to his creatures. God's ultimate inscrutability does not prevent Paul from trying to make sense of what is happening, using his reason and his imagination. The biblical ideas of election and remnant provide material for an argument denying that the word of God has failed (9.6). Divine election (as the chosen people know well) marks out some and not others—Jacob not Esau. Fair play is not an issue, as the hardening of Pharaoh shows.

Paul's claim that not all Israel are really Israel is an answer of sorts to the problem of majority Israel's unbelief. But the point added in vv. 11-12 is superfluous to this argument and suggests that Paul's mind is really elsewhere. The choice between Jacob and Esau was not made on a basis of anything they had done, good or evil. God's decision was based on election, as any Calvinist would agree. Paul's phrase 'good or evil' suggests that 'works' are moral deeds, but it does not require that interpretation. The phrase could simply underline Paul's 'anything'. Election depended on absolutely nothing that they had done. The phrase 'not from works' must be understood by reference to other occurrences of the word in this epistle (4.2; 9.32; 11.6, cf. 3.20, 27-28; 4.6, cf. Gal. 2.16; 3.2, 5, 10). Even when trying to explain majority Israel's unbelief Paul is wanting to advance his underlying argument that relationship with God is based on God's calling and faith, not on observance of Torah.

This argument surfaces in the second main division of Romans 9–11, summarized above, pp. 53-54. Scriptural quotations are used to explain that what has happened is a fulfilment of prophecy. The division between those who recognize what God is now doing and those who take offence (cf. 1 Cor. 1.23) and reject it occurs over their response to Christ, and this is vividly expressed by identifying Christ with the 'stone' in Isa. 8.14 and 28.16 (Rom. 9.33, echoed at 10.11—and followed by 1 Pet. 2.6, 8). This typological use of Scripture (cf. 1 Cor. 10.4) provides a christological base for what follows: a quotation of Lev. 18.5 (found also at Gal. 3.12) and a midrash on Deut. 30.12-14.

The difficulty of this passage is signalled by the endless

arguments over whether Christ the *telos* of (the) law means end in the sense of termination or goal. Most commentators think that Paul is contrasting a right relationship to God based on Torah observance (v. 5) with that based on faith in Christ (v. 6), corresponding to the contrast drawn in v. 3 between the righteousness of God and their own righteousness (cf. Phil. 3.9). Gal. 3.11-12 rather supports this view. However, v. 4 is ambiguous and perhaps intentionally so. Only the slightly different phrase in Phil. 3.9 and the use of Lev. 18.5 in Gal. 3.12 tell against Paul here speaking positively of the law. In its Romans context v. 4 seems to favour a positive sense for law, as well as for Christ and righteousness. This implies the translation 'goal'—and that makes it hard to read the explanatory v. 5 in negative terms, or v. 6 as a contrast to v. 5. That 'But' could be translated 'And': thus Moses associates the law with salvation (v. 5 and cf. 7.10), and Christian faith-righteousness (v. 6) is promised in the law, for example, Deuteronomy 30. It is hard for crypto-Marcionites to read this passage in a way that weakens their antithesis between Law and Gospel, but it may be right.

When Paul wants to express his negative thesis (not by Torah observance) in Romans he prefers to speak of works, or 'works of law' (3.20, 28) rather than 'the law'. To speak of Torah absolutely in this context might threaten Scripture itself. It is thus quite possible that this passage (v. 5) is more positive about the law and more conciliatory towards Jewish Christians than has often been thought. Since Paul does in fact retain the law as part of his Scripture, and still believes it is God's law (even though Gentiles need not fulfil the requirements of circumcision, food laws and sabbath) one would expect to find him redefining it as a story of faith rather than a collection of works or ritual requirements. That may be what is happening here, as perhaps at 3.27 (above p. 32).

In the present context Paul at least expresses himself ambiguously and is willing to be understood to be speaking of the law in this positive way. He does not here press the antithesis that (as Phil. 3.9 shows) stands at the heart of his own theology and missionary practice, though he constantly echoes it. Instead he uses Scripture to support his positive assertions about Christ, Christian preaching, and faith. It is not necessary to bring Christ down from heaven or up from the dead because he is alive and present in Christian preaching. Acknowledging this truth draws believers into a right relationship with God and will lead to salvation. Again Paul's major concern breaks through in v. 12 when he repeats the word used at 3.22 that there is no distinction between Jew and Greek (cf. 2.11). Christ is Lord of all, and calling on him is all that is necessary (v. 13, quoting Joel 2.32). The implication is again that circumcision and food laws are not required of Gentile converts.

The causal connections between God's sending missionaries out to the ends of the (Gentile) world, their proclamation of Christ, hearing it, faith, confession, and salvation, are joyfully celebrated with the help of quotations from Isaiah and the Psalter. The problem of Israel's refusal is spliced into this, also through quotations of Scripture which in Paul's view prophesies both Israel's disobedient rejection and the Gentile mission. In v. 19 Deut. 32.21 is quoted to adumbrate ch. 11.

The theme of this third division of Romans 9–11 is introduced in the words of Ps. 94.14 noted above. The remnant argument introduced at 9.27 is repeated, now quoting Elijah at 1 Kgs 19.10, 14 and God's reply, and relating this to God's election by grace in the present situation. Again the central antithesis of the epistle (faith and works) is expressed (v. 6), slightly varied by a reference to grace rather than faith, but containing a 'no longer by works'. That this is scarcely appropriate to the Elijah situation is irrelevant to Paul who is thinking of the present. A kind of sense is made of the blindness of Israel by its having been prophesied, and the Psalter's imprecations are again invoked as at 3.10-18. If Paul has to be negative about Israel, so was David, and nobody questions David's loyalty.

The solution which Paul offers to the problem of Israel's unbelief is not based on biblical prophecy. His own Christian prophecy, or inspiration, allows him access to God's 'mystery' (v. 25). This is simply confirmed with a composite quotation from Isa. 59.20-21 and 27.9. The same book (40.13) provides material for the final peroration to this section of the epistle.

Paul's Use of Scripture

A brief survey cannot do full justice to all the Septuagintal vocabulary scattered throughout the epistle (e.g. in chs. 1–2). Romans is more saturated in the Old Testament than any book in the New Testament except Revelation. Some narrowly argumentative functions have been identified, especially in ch. 4, but the support Scripture gives to Paul's proclamation is generally more confirmatory than probative. Quotations and allusions evoke common ground, and run deeper than his particular arguments and reassurances. Given the resonance that Scripture has for Paul and some of his hearers, quoting or echoing it draws himself and them into what he is saying about God in ways that are characteristic of religious discourse. But before this is explored further another main source of Paul's thought and language must be considered.

Paul knows who God is from his Jewish upbringing and training which was based on Scripture. But recent events (twenty-odd years ago) have drastically revised his understanding of what God is now doing and what he himself has been called to do. What later Christians call the Old Testament was not, therefore, the only or most important source of his religious life. The first disciples' proclamation of Jesus, summarized in the creed quoted at 1 Cor. 15.3-5, had made possible Paul's new understanding of what God was now doing. He claims to know Jesus by revelation (1 Cor. 9.1; 15.8) and even to have received his eucharistic traditions 'from the Lord' (1 Cor. 11.23), but the revelation and faith event in which he became convinced that it was in Christ that God was reconciling the world to himself was only possible because traditions identifying this Messiah Jesus were available.

Paul provides remarkably few indications of how much he knew about the historical figure Jesus. He occasionally quotes or echoes a saying of Jesus (e.g. Rom. 12.14) and 'the cross' refers to the historical event by which above all Jesus is identified, but Paul's focus is usually on the risen Lord. It is therefore not surprising that some of the most important things he says about Jesus come in the form of quotations or echoes of liturgical material, that is, creeds and hymns. These can sometimes be recognized (i.e. hypotheses can be ventured) from their carefully balanced clauses, vocabulary untypical of Paul himself, and formal characteristics such as introduction by a relative pronoun ('who'), a participle, or a 'that'.

1.3-4

This is an obvious example. It was noted above (p. 78) that it would have been politic of Paul to demonstrate at the outset that he shared the faith of his Jewish-Christian hearers by quoting a creed with which they will have been familiar. If he himself added the phrase 'in power' to avoid the hint of 'adoptionism' (Jesus promoted from humanity to divinity at the resurrection), as some commentators think, that shows these formulae were less dogmatically fixed than later creeds. Unlike Matthew, Paul himself elsewhere makes no use of the royal messianic title 'son of David'. Addressing Gentiles, 'Lord' and 'Son of God' communicated more; even 'Christ' (messiah, 66 times in Rom.) is usually (lacking the definite article) weakened by Paul from a title to a proper name.

The exegesis of v. 4 is difficult: the verb could mean either 'designated' or 'appointed'. 'Spirit of holiness' is a Hebrew idiom and presumably means the Holy Spirit, God in action who is seen as instrumental in the eschatological event of resurrection. This formula, like Paul himself at 1 Cor. 15.20, sees Jesus' resurrection as the start of the general resurrection expected by many Jews.

The formula 'Seed (i.e. Son) of David—Son of God' was perhaps based on 2 Sam. 7.14 where God promises to be a Father to David's son Solomon. That verse was interpreted eschatologically at Qumran. The phrase 'Son of God' has also been found (4Q246) but is not a messianic title there.

4.25

As the epistle almost certainly begins with a liturgical couplet, so the first major section probably ends with one. 4.25 looks like an afterthought. It fits the context well, but is not strictly part of the preceding argument. Rather it reinforces the christological base of the argument that a right relationship to God is through faith (in Christ). It is introduced with the relative pronoun 'who' (cf. Phil. 2.6; Col. 1.15; 1 Tim. 3.16, all probably quotations of christological hymns). The couplet is balanced; and the thought, separating the functions of the death and resurrection of Jesus, is not quite Pauline. The vocabulary probably echoes Isaiah 53, the Suffering Servant Song which was perhaps a source of early Jewish Christianity's theological ideas of justification (cf. Isa. 53.11) and the sacrificial death of Christ. Paul himself uses the rare word translated 'justification' or acquittal only here and at 5.18.

3.24-25

This more difficult passage carries the additional burden of subsequent doctrinal reflection on the atonement (see below, pp. 99-100). Its untypical language and heavily overloaded phrases are best explained on the hypothesis that Paul is quoting or echoing one or possibly two liturgical formulae and adding comments of his own to interpret them. Like 1.3 the formula in v. 24 begins with a participle, but the vocabulary is Pauline. The present participle (passive) of 'to put right' is untypical, and 'redemption' is used slightly differently from 8.23, which refers to a still future event. Even so the case for a pre-Pauline formula in v. 24 is weak.

It is much stronger in v. 25 which begins with a relative pronoun linking it to this context. The much debated word translated 'propitiation' in the AV, but 'expiation' in most modern translations is without parallel in Paul. 'In (or 'by') his blood' surely belongs with expiation, suggesting that 'through faith' is Paul's addition. Despite the Book of Common Prayer, a 'bloody sacrifice appropriated by faith' (cf. 5.9) is more Pauline and more intelligible than 'faith in his blood'. Two more un-Pauline words can be translated either to 'show' or to 'prove' ('demonstrate' catches the ambiguity) and either 'passing over' or 'forgiveness'.

Verse 26 looks like Paul's own parallel formulation to v. 25, showing how he understands it. Here God's 'righteousness' means God's saving action, as at 1.17 and 3.21, whereas in v. 25, like the less typical occurrence at 3.5, it seems to refer to a quality in God. The history of misunderstanding

v. 25 arises from taking that quality to be 'justice' in the Greek sense of 'rendering to each his (or her) due'. That suggested that the point of Christ's sacrificial death was to satisfy the requirements of God's justice (that sin be punished) by substituting a victim who could suffer vicariously for the sins of the whole world—including those 'committed beforehand' but 'passed over' (temporarily) 'in the patience of God'.

That surely is not how Paul or his predecessors understood the sacrificial death of Christ. At Rom. 3.5 (and often in the Psalter) God's 'righteousness' means his faithfulness to his covenant. Here too the phrase has to do with God's mercy, not some requirement of an impersonal divine justice. God passed over sins committed in the past, that is, did not punish them at once, in order to give time for repentance (cf. 2.5). His present initiative in Christ provides a means of atonement, not by a death that can satisfy the moral order through an overdue act of retribution, but (according to the Jewish Christian theology of v. 25) by providing a sacrifice (cf. Gen. 22.8; Rom. 8.32) to renew the covenant. And (adds Paul in v. 26, picking up v. 21) establishing at the present time a way to salvation. The righteous and faithful God creates this new relationship through Jesus-faith (or through the faithfulness of Jesus).

1 Cor. 15.3 shows that (Jewish) Christians very early interpreted the death of Jesus as a sacrifice, and that idea is present here too ('offer' as well as 'expiation in or through his blood') and is implied at 4.25. That is, however, different from some substitutionary theories of atonement. Substitution takes place in sacrifice, but there is no idea of God punishing an innocent victim. Rather, God accepts the offering of the worshipper. The 'catholic oblation' of Christ, the one true perfect sacrifice, is explored in the epistle to the Hebrews, and can find support in these pre-Pauline Jewish-Christian ideas. The same cannot be said for atonement theories based on a misunderstanding of Paul's use of the word 'righteousness'. The danger in translating it 'justice' is that it will be wrongly contrasted with God's mercy. For Paul, as in Psalm 85, God's righteousness and mercy coincide.

The controversy over whether v. 25 means that an angry

God is propitiated—placated, as some evangelicals think—or
that sins are expiated—covered, dealt with—as in Heb. 2.17
and (probably) 1 Jn 2.2 where similar words are used, cannot
be settled on lexical grounds. Following Luther, who saw a
possible allusion to Exodus 25 and 37, and Leviticus 16, the
AV translates *hilastērion* 'mercy-seat'—the lid of the ark on
which the blood was sprinkled, that is, the place of expiation.
But that implies the cross, not Jesus himself, and 'means of
expiation' is probably right. Paul himself shows little interest
in the mechanics of atonement. His emphasis falls on the
situation before and after the faith response to what God has
done in Christ: the human plight (enslaved, guilty, at enmity
with God) and the reality of redemption, liberation, acquittal,
reconciliation, peace, a right relationship with God, incorpo-
ration in Christ, new creation, new hope.

It is probable that Paul is also quoting or echoing an early
Christian creed that 'Jesus is Lord' at 10.9, where he uses
the word 'confess'. The same phrase occurs in 1 Cor. 12.3, in
what looks like a formula, and it is included in the famous
Christ hymn at Phil. 2.11. This confession is also echoed at 1
Cor. 8.6. However, it is necessary to be cautious as we know
very little about early Christian liturgy beyond the practice
of baptism and celebration of the Lord's Supper.

Paul refers to the rite of initiation at 6.3-5, but his 'do you
not know' may be rhetorical and need not imply that his
theology of baptism was familiar to his hearers. It seems
clear that early Christianity was quite creative in developing
the language of worship, and that this was one context in
which its theology, especially its christology, developed (cf.
Pliny's letter to the emperor Trajan in 112 CE about the
Christians singing hymns to Jesus as to God). It would not be
surprising if Paul echoes much more early Christian liturgical material (e.g. in ch. 8 and in his other doxologies) than
we can now detect with confidence. It is also likely that a
powerful phrase maker like Paul, no less than a literary
artist like Luke, may have himself contributed to the development of early Christian liturgy before writing Romans.

More important than identifying possibilities in the hope of
clarifying pre-Pauline ideas is considering what all this
intertextual use of Scripture and tradition tells us about the

nature of the epistle's talk of God. Religious belief in and talk of God is generally rooted in an already existing religious tradition. The reality and identity of God is already presupposed when some new experience clarifies, develops, or corrects earlier beliefs (cf. Exod. 3.14; 6.3). Paul presupposes who God is and where and how God is known. He believes that Scripture identifies the God of Israel as God of all and that it supports his convictions about God's revelation for all in the death and resurrection of the Messiah Jesus, God's present activity in the Spirit, and the future expectation. Jewish Scripture and Jewish-Christian traditions about Jesus are necessary to express and communicate his gospel message (which is also a vehicle) of what God is now doing. The intertextuality of Romans is an indication not only of theological argument on the basis of Scripture, but that Paul speaks more directly of God here than elsewhere. God, the gospel of God, is everywhere presupposed in Paul's epistles, but is the theme only of Romans. That gives this epistle its special place in Christianity, after the four gospels.

5

THE RELIGIOUS
LANGUAGE OF ROMANS

To UNDERSTAND A LETTER the more that can be known about
the writer's purposes and relationship to the recipients the
better. Romans gives mixed signals about the situation
addressed and Paul's precise purposes, but the similarities to
Galatians and the differences from that earlier epistle
allowed us in Chapter 3 to frame a hypothesis to explain this
web of celebration, exposition, argument, and exhortation,
which have enthralled but also puzzled later readers.

Assuming the modern debate has brought the text into
historical focus we are better placed to understand it than
anyone since its original hearers. Yet the kind of understanding which that yields is quite superficial, not plumbing
the depths of this classic of religious literature.
Reconstructing the history of Paul and early Christianity
clears away some of the mists that time lays around any
ancient monument, but it has only a supporting role with
respect to the kind of engagement which this letter calls for.
We may prefer not to hear its challenge as addressed to us
personally, but to ignore its own religious aims would be to
trivialize it, and to overlook its subsequent impact would be
to miss much of what makes it worth studying.

The approach which our opening chapter proposed as a
way of grasping the meaning and significance of this work
without committing ourselves to its truth or falsity was to
read it in terms of an informed understanding of religion.
Most readers will draw that from their grasp of their own

religious tradition in the first place, but can sharpen their perception by considering other traditions and using whatever analytic tools are available from the humanities and social sciences.

Religion

There are many competing definitions of religion but most of them speak of worshipping God or the gods and recognize the symbolic character of much religious language. Some explain the social functions of rituals, doctrines, and lifestyles in terms of the meanings and values these provide for those who participate. When students of religion ask what these strange beliefs and practices mean for those involved they find more to this universal human phenomenon than meets the untrained eye.

Much of a new religion's vocabulary is drawn from the already existing religious tradition. This may be stretched and bent and broken under the pressure of new experience but new insights need a language and existing terms provide a starting point. It is therefore vital to investigate where possible any new religion's relationship to its historical and religious matrix.

Not that Paul realized he was helping shape a new religion. He was born a Jew and remained one religiously as well as ethnically, even though in around 33 CE he moved from his pharisaic practice to a still Jewish messianic sect. He spoke of this as a call (Gal. 1.15), analogous to the call of some biblical prophets; and like some of theirs it involved a call vision (1 Cor. 9.1; 15.8-9). Like Jeremiah (1.5) Paul was directed to the Gentiles, who are again addressed in Isa. 49.1, which he also echoes.

Paul's call to be an apostle to the Gentiles involved a conviction that God was accepting them without the works of the law. Though he did not call this a conversion, it involved a dramatic religious reorientation. A break with the synagogue was inevitable, as he acknowledges by founding new congregations. But he denies that God has cast off his people (Rom. 11.1), and he expected them shortly to be brought in at the consummation (11.25-32). Meanwhile neither he himself, nor other Jews who were persuaded that Jesus was the

Messiah, thought they had changed religions. They continued to worship the same God and to read the same Scriptures, though interpreted in new ways in the light of what God was now doing.

Scripture

Paul's participation in a religious tradition, visible in his use of his Scriptures (see previous chapter) is thus the key to his religious language. Scripture is not only the main source of his words and ideas and beliefs and assumptions but part of a functioning religious system within which Paul's whole talk of God makes sense. His preaching and teaching and living the gospel depend on an interaction between tradition (notably Scripture) and experience. The tradition was not just a source of ideas and convictions and warrants but an active volcano of religious faith and life in which the experience of individuals is constantly being processed. Without the backing of Scripture and religious practice Paul would not be a religious teacher speaking of the God of Israel but a freebooter. A religious philosopher's claim to wisdom and insight may also draw on a tradition. Paul's claim to revelation is as different from that as religion is different from philosophy. That his gospel was promised by God beforehand through his prophets in holy Scriptures (1.2) and witnessed to by the law and the prophets (3.21) is more than a supporting argument. Without this presupposition of God at work and known in Judah (Ps. 76.1) there is no Pauline gospel.

The biblical traditions about Adam, Abraham, Moses, David and Elijah provide Paul with specific arguments and a general support for his claim to be loyal to Israel's heritage (9.1-5; 10.1; 11.1). But the problem addressed in chs. 9–11 shows that more is at stake. The problem is not 'the problem of Israel', that is, why many failed to believe. Paul regrets this but finds it prophesied. The real problem would be if God had rejected his people (11.1) because that would imply that the word of God had failed (9.6). Paul defends the validity of Scripture because he believes it is true. We may add that the logic of his own discourse requires this. There is no gospel without Scripture, no new religious talk of God without an already existing tradition bearing an active religious life that already believes and talks of God.

When Paul speaks of God he is not a philosopher of religion, even though he can on occasion argue his case from monotheism (3.29-30). God is the one who is known to him from tradition (especially his scriptural tradition) and experience, and worshipped partly through the language of tradition. Tradition precedes and gives shape to experience. Sometimes religious experience, including the response to God we call worship, can precede a knowledge of a tradition, but when powerful and influential believers revise or reshape their tradition they usually know it well.

Paul did not think he had changed religions. He was still a loyal Jew. But in another sense he had changed his religion rather drastically. When he sees Scripture promising and bearing witness to the decisive saving event, the dawn of the age to come, in the sending of God's Son (Rom. 8.3; Gal. 4.6) and his death and resurrection, it is his Lord Jesus Messiah, no longer the Torah, that is the focus of his knowledge and love of God (cf. Gal. 2.20; 1 Cor. 8.3; 13.12; Phil. 3.8-10).

Gospel

Paul designates his new focus on the death and resurrection of Christ (1 Cor. 15.3-4) 'the gospel' (*evangel*—used absolutely 24 times in the authentic epistles) or gospel of God, or of Christ, or concerning his Son (see p. 17). This 'message' word, good news, includes information (1.9; 10.9), but for Paul it refers to an event of God's power. It heralds salvation for all who accept as Lord the Jesus who is made present by the word of proclamation. Paul sees in this human word the vehicle of God's creative word (cf. 1 Thess. 2.13; 2 Cor. 5.20; Rom. 10.8-17).

He probably chose this noun on the basis of the Septuagintal verb 'to proclaim glad tidings' (*evangelize*). That verb is found six times in Isaiah 40–66 (quoted by Paul at 10.15). In the Psalter the verb is associated with 'righteousness', 'word', or 'salvation'. Paul himself uses it a further 18 times, sometimes with the noun. The noun is insignifcant in the LXX. It was also used in pagan religious contexts (as is evidenced in an inscription found at Priene and dated to

9 BCE) and this will have enhanced its intelligibility. But it is the biblical bells rung by Paul's vocabulary which carry the presumption he is speaking of God, the God already known in Judah.

Paul's religion had always consisted in an obedient response, as a member of God's covenant people, to God's revelation of a holy will and plan for the world and human life. His refocusing his trust and obedience in the blinding light of the revelation of the knowledge of the glory of God in the face of Jesus Messiah (cf. 2 Cor. 4.6) led him to speak of his recently crucified and vindicated contemporary in the new ways advocated by earlier disciples of Jesus.

Christology

Paul's linguistic creativity is not so apparent in his christological language as elsewhere. Traces of other early Christian thought about Jesus are probably visible in quotations of liturgical material in the epistles, as in the traditions used in Acts and the Synoptic Gospels. At least some of the titles applied to Jesus were used in Aramaic before Paul wrote (cf. 1 Cor. 16.22).

The Hebrew word messiah (*maṣiaḥ*) or 'anointed one' becomes *Christos* in Paul's Greek. It has usually become a name but occasionally the definite article makes it a title (Rom. 9.3, 5; 15.3, 7, 19; 16.16) and the frequent word order 'Christ Jesus' echoes that too. As a 'son of David' this eschatological agent was expected on earth as a human, and even 'son of God' could have this human sense. But in the light of the resurrection Jesus' followers also soon thought of him in divine or heavenly terms. The Johannine Christians, for example, later expelled from their synagogue as heretics, were perhaps influenced by Jewish speculation about angels. Paul echoes the 'Son of David' tradition at 1.3 and in his 'Gentiles' quotation of Isa. 11.10 at 15.12, but unlike Matthew and Luke he does not use this title, probably because he has so little to say about Jesus' earthly life prior to the crucifixion.

The most original and interesting christological idea in Romans does, however, allude to Jesus' humanity (as does 8.3, contrary to the Arians' interpretation of 'likeness'). Like

1 Cor. 15.21-22 (cf. 45-47) and probably Phil. 2.6-11, Rom. 5.12-19 interprets Christ's saving work by contrasting his obedience with Adam's disobedience. But Paul is not here clarifying Christ's status so much as that of Christians. Christ is a corporate and representative figure for Paul, and we shall return to this shortly, but first the other titles taken over from early Christian tradition must be noted.

In the Gentile mission titles such as Lord and Son of God would have a divine flavour (cf. 1 Cor. 8.6) *Kyrios* is very common in Paul's writings (e.g. in variants of 'Jesus Christ our Lord' at 5.11, 21; 6.23; 7.25; 8.39 etc.), and Son of God occurs fifteen times (e.g. Rom. 1.3-4, 9).

These two titles of exaltation show that Paul's religious focus is on the risen Lord. Jesus has come to this position through his life and death. At the heart of Paul's religion therefore is a narrative which relates God and Jesus. If 'myth' is defined non-pejoratively as a narrative of God or the gods the category is applicable here. A recently executed historical figure is spoken of and historical fact therefore essential, but what Paul had to say about Jesus is set in a framework of his Scripture-based talk of God.

Atonement

That combination of history and theology is clear in the way Paul interprets the death of Jesus. Unlike 1 Cor. 1.18, Romans does not summarize the narrative by making a historical reference to 'the cross' a symbol of the whole, but here as always he says more about the death of Jesus than his life.

Like the church before him (1 Cor. 15.3) he interprets this in sacrificial terms ('for'). These were so much a part of his Jewish thinking that he could make of them a metaphor for the Christian life (12.1) and his own missionary activity (15.16). More centrally, sacrifice is implied in another older formula quoted at 4.25 (above p. 89). This echoes Isa. 53.5, 10, 12 to suggest that it was 'according to the Scriptures' (1 Cor. 15.3) that Christ 'was handed over *for* our transgressions.' Like Abraham God 'did not spare his own Son, but gave him up for us all' (8.32). At 3.25, again probably echoing older formulae, Paul says that a sacrifice initiated by God was a means of expiation (blotting out sin), or alternatively propitiation (placating God), or atonement (*hilastērion*) in or through his (Christ's) blood, and at 5.9 he says we were justified in or by his blood, that is, sacrificial death (see below, p. 118).

Whether *hilastērion* (above p. 92) means the lid of the ark on which sacrificial blood was scattered (in Hebrew the *kapporeth*) as 19 times in Exodus and Leviticus, or whether (as is more likely) a more general reference is intended, the interpretation is probably sacrificial. Paul (like John) could understand the death of Jesus at Passover in terms of the sacrificial lambs being killed then (1 Cor. 5.7); a further echo of Isaiah 53 is also present (v. 7). Like the rest of the early church he interprets the death of Christ sacrificially at the eucharist (1 Cor. 10.16; 11.24-26), though the covenant Paul sees this establishing is the new eschatological covenant of Jer. 31.31. Others (cf. Mk 14.24) perhaps saw it as re-establishing the Mosaic covenant (cf. Exod. 24.8), as in the tradition behind Rom. 3.25 (above p. 91).

If such ideas are foreign to most modern Western readers that does not answer the question of their importance for Paul. Their relation to Paul's other language about salvation will be considered below, but already the contexts in Romans suggest that his main interest in this language was to make clear that God's pro-active (3.25) love for the world is made visible in the one 'who loved me and gave himself for me' (Gal. 2.20, cf. Rom. 5.7-8).

Resurrection

Jesus, then, was the Son 'sent' by God (8.3), not spared (8.32), but set forth as an atoning sacrifice (3.25) and then raised from the dead (10.9; 4.25, cf. 1.4). The phrase 'Son of God' later became the leading metaphor relating Jesus to God. Equally clearly metaphorical is the language of resurrection (getting up or standing up), taken over from Jewish prayer (cf. Rom. 4.17 and above p. 34) and eschatological expectations (e.g. Dan. 12.2) and from previous Jewish-Christian tradition (1 Cor. 15.3-5; Rom. 1.4) to express God's vindication of Jesus following his shameful death (cf. Rom. 4.25). To make sense of this language today it is not enough either to acknowledge the metaphor or to identify its background. Something more has informed Christian appropriation of it: believing the miracle. The empirical reality of the event itself has been presupposed and this has controlled the way this metaphor has been understood. Literal interpretation has seemed the surest way of insisting on the ontological reality that Christian experience has, from soon after the crucifixion, claimed for this mystery or divine event.

Whether that is right or wrong, it is not the only possibility. The supernatural assumption was challenged in the eighteenth century by deists like Reimarus who denied both the event and the inferences drawn from it. The evidence does not compel belief and even Christians who insist on a mysterious divine event vindicating Jesus may be agnostic about its precise character. In any case the figurative character, rhetorical power, and religious and social functions of Paul's language can be understood without prejudice to its truth or correspondence with reality.

Paul and the others believed that God had raised Jesus from the dead (10.9), but 1 Corinthians 15 shows that he did not think of this mysterious divine event as a resuscitation. Neither did he see it as demonstrating the truth of his gospel, despite 1 Cor. 15.6. In his view people come to faith by responding to Christian proclamation (10.14-17) not through rational historical argument. Proclamation consists in testimony, where believers pick up others' confessions of Christian faith and make them the fabric of their own faith and experience, and so a language for communicating it.

Paul's religious language evidently made good sense to some of his Christian contemporaries and successors. Those who do not share his cultural assumptions find it obscure. Paul's rhetoric may, like poetry, communicate before it is understood, but a conceptual framework that fits both the religious language of the text and the assumptions of modern readers should make it more intelligible.

The traditional Christian doctrinal framework still functions in this way for many readers, providing a grid through which they make sense of his thought. Other believers are less comfortable with that scheme and prefer to make sense of this text through a conceptual framework shared with uncommitted colleagues. Clarifying the text's message through new categories may help communicate it afresh.

A proposal arising from the symbolic character of much religious language is to understand Paul's in terms of his projecting a symbolic world. He is not describing empirical reality, even though in his letters he is socially engaged and often alludes to his own and his hearers' historical situation. Neither is he developing a philosophical or theological system, even though his ideas and arguments occasionally echo popular philosophy (e.g. 2.14-15; 7.18-19) and were later built into theological systems. But all religious ideas and practices encapsulate human meanings in symbolic form and Paul articulates a vision of the world and human life under God.

A System of Symbols

Regardless of how far his original readers accepted or modern readers adopt his configuration, the web that Paul weaves can be made more intelligible by studying a range of religious texts. Theories of religion offer tools for analysis here, sharpening the eye for aspects of the data. But they can also tempt interpreters to press the data into an inappropriate mould. Attempts to explain religions away as purely the products of psychological or socio-economic conditions, for example, are reductionist. Freudians and Marxists are right to see some correlation between influential symbols and personal and social experience, but their causal explanations short-circuit the complexities of our human worlds and prejudge religious claims to truth. It is possible to share their descriptions of the symbolic language of religion while rejecting their denials of its truth and value.

In Paul's symbol system the narrative of Jesus' incarnation ('sent'), death and resurrection is part of the larger biblical story of God's engagement with the world. That is not baldly asserted as in the creeds, but is everywhere assumed. God is creator (Rom. 4.17; 1 Cor. 8.6) and the eschatological future described in traditional imagery in 1 Thess. 4.13–5.4 and 1 Corinthians 15 is evoked in Rom. 8.18-23, and assumed at 13.11. Between these points is the history of salvation discussed in Romans 4 and 9–11. It is less prominent in Paul than in Luke. Paul's eschatological frame of reference is focused more sharply on the death and resurrection of Jesus and his symbolic world can be depicted as well in spatial as in linear temporal terms.

(Level 1) God. We can arrange on three levels the symbols and metaphors that point participants to the reality they worship and so interpret for them their own human life. God transcends everything and human language is inadequate to ultimate reality. But when worshippers turn towards God or make themselves present to the presence of God they need a focus for their religious activity. Jews and Christians and some others use inherited symbols which (they believe) mediate that gracious reality and enable them to know and love God. The presumed reality as such is not a human construct and so has no place on our symbolic map, but our pictures and ideas of God are thought to reflect it and so constitute the top level on the map.

The metaphors and analogies which point to the reality of God are the apex of the worshipper's symbolic world. The way this is formed, however, makes level 2, the decisive event of revelation, the heart and centre of a religious symbol system. Something of God, says Paul, may be known indirectly through the created order (Rom 1.19-20), but God is named in Jewish and Christian and some other worshipping communities in the language of tradition and on the basis of some presumed revelation event. Most people's sense of God is shaped by a tradition of past revelatory events. This makes possible the recognition or reception of the new and decisive revelation which proves foundational for a new religious community.

Paul knew who God is, and was able to respond to God, through the resources of his Jewish religious tradition, especially its Scriptures. Only on that basis could he recognize the crucified and risen Jesus as the decisive revelation of that one and the same God. But once recognized as such this event has repercussions on the symbol 'God' (level 1). As the God and Father of our Lord Jesus Christ the God of Abraham and Isaac and Jacob is known differently from before. The symbols of our level 1 are modified or given new content by the decisive revelation (described on level 2) of the God they evoke or refer to.

Converts are very likely to be negative about what they have left behind and Paul's present convictions imply a negative judgment on some aspects of his former practice, but even Paul (unlike Marcion) is fundamentally positive about the old (Rom. 3.2; 9.4-5). He still accepts the relative validity of the biblical oracles while reserving absolute validity for the related revelation in Christ.

(Level 2) Revelation. This level of our map or model contains the symbols which represent the central revelatory event. It therefore largely determines how God is worshipped and understood, and also determines the implications that follow for human life and community. These are given symbolic form on level 3 of our map, deriving from the revelation event. To be human is to belong to the physical world as a biological organism, but also to create symbols which express meaning and value. *'Homo sapiens'* is *homo symbolicus* (or *symboloficiens*)—a symbol-making animal. Everyone lives on some level 3, making sense of life, however fragmentarily. Some inhabit elaborate symbol systems, whether religious (i.e. including levels 2 and 1) or not. These systems are constructed by humans, but the poets, apostles and prophets most responsible for religious developments think they are somehow responding to the mystery and that their actions and writings correspond to the reality that is disclosing itself to them.

Paul says so little about Jesus of Nazareth himself that it would be easy in a description of his symbolic world to reduce the revelation to a point, the in-breaking of the new age in the event of Jesus' death and resurrection. Or since for Paul the revelation does not draw its content from Jesus' personality one might suppose that this must be drawn from the common stock of Jewish expectations or pagan ideas. Paul made use of these linguistic resources, but our comments on christology and resurrection implied a distinction between his language and what it refers to. The decisive revelation of God is located in a person, a person identified by his human life and death, and allegedly made known to Paul in his risen life. That belief might be dismissed as illusion, but to Paul it was unquestionably true, corresponding to reality. Talk of Paul's symbolic world would therefore miss his passionate commitment and engagement if it did not consider *how* he inhabited it and how the *person* Jesus is alive to him.

It would be possible to unpack all Paul's theology in terms of what he means by faith and its object. Any talk of 'revelation' requires a correlative term describing its appropriation or reception. That might be seeing, knowing, intuiting or believing. For Paul the essential term is faith. It describes a personal relationship of trust and confidence, joy and yearning (5.2-3; 8.18ff.), response to God's love (Gal. 2.20).

God was already symbolized in personal terms in the religious tradition. Where God is known pre-eminently in the crucified Messiah Jesus who is alive and reigns, the personal character of the revelation and religious responses must be insisted on, even though the nature of Paul's letter (unlike Augustine's *Confessions* or some of the Psalms) allows it expression only in passages such as 5.1-11 and 8.31-39. To acknowledge God's revelation in Christ is to cleave to a loving Lord. Romans says nothing about the rituals by which this relationship is sustained and nurtured, notably the eucharist (cf. 1 Cor. 10.16-24; 11.17-34). Interpreters dare not overlook what is simply presupposed.

(Level 3) Community. Religions generate and sustain community through institutions and practices and through moral and metaphysical ideas. Worshippers may find themselves empowered to make their social organizations and personal lives conform better to the ideas and ideals expressed in their symbols. Paul, of course, thought his religious language referred to the reality he called God, and millions have agreed with him on the basis of their own religious experience. Such convictions are neither confirmed nor challenged here. Our task is to *describe* Paul's system not to evaluate it. Whether it truly mediates the reality of God cannot be answered from the outside, though observers can comment on its good and bad effects. Most people begin their human quest for meaning by taking on trust the guidance of some

tradition and parent or teacher, and acknowledge its truth in a constantly renewed decision and confession (10.9) which Paul calls the obedience of faith (1.5).

Religious symbol systems sustain community by rituals and beliefs and patterns of behaviour. Paul is clear about the purchase his religious practice has on individual lives and social reality, but he does not explain this. The true believer does not wait for a theory of religious practice. Theory is often a sign that a system is in need of support. But theory can also arise from a confidence that religious truth can be communicated in the language of new cultural fashions. Rahner's theory, for example, that symbols participate in the reality they express (*Theological Investigations IV*) cannot compel assent, but has been found illuminating by some and can help others to see what kind of claim is being made by those who inhabit a religion.

Without thinking in the terms borrowed here for purpose of analysis, Paul assumed that his religious language expressed and supported an authentic relationship with the one God now decisively revealed in Jesus Christ. Personal value, meaning and fulfilment—no less than social integration—stem from that root relationship of the creature with the Creator which we shall identify as the main concern of Paul's religious language. Since Paul himself thought his symbols took participants into the reality of God an analyst may speak of his 'symbolic realism'. That label warns against interpreting his language as 'mere' metaphors, less real than the empirical world. For Paul, God is the most really real, and the revelation derives from that. The symbols which express humanity's fractured and restored relationship to God are for him more real than for modern empiricists. We may or may not be persuaded by his rhetoric, but as students of religion must try to see things from the believer's perspective.

The model we are proposing can be represented as follows, with (A) in brackets because some of Paul's readers can deny or ignore the reality of God, whereas they cannot deny symbols or the natural world. To be human is to live on the symbolic (B) and physical (C) planes, but not as a Cartesian ghost in a material machine. Paul's belief that it is the

Creator who rescues humanity, giving life to dead bodies
(4.17) excludes metaphysical dualism. We do not have bodies;
we are bodies and must glorify God in our body (1 Cor. 6.20),
no less than being renewed in mind (Rom. 12.2). Paul sometimes uses dualistic language, but this must be interpreted
in the light of his basic Jewish convictions about God and
the world. Humans are a unity of our B and C, whether
their symbol system (B) contains levels 1 and 2 or not. If it
does, then this will control level 3. Understanding the
symbols by which Paul articulates human life and community will involve seeing how his level 3 flows from his levels
2 and 1. Understanding his religion will involve seeing how
the whole symbolic world shapes and motivates a personal
and social life in which worship and ethics coincide (cf.
12.1-2).

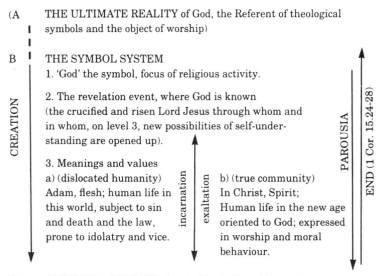

(A   THE ULTIMATE REALITY of God, the Referent of theological
       symbols and the object of worship)

B   THE SYMBOL SYSTEM
       1. 'God' the symbol, focus of religious activity.

       2. The revelation event, where God is known
       (the crucified and risen Lord Jesus through whom and
       in whom, on level 3, new possibilities of self-under-
       standing are opened up).

       3. Meanings and values
       a) (dislocated humanity)   b) (true community)
       Adam, flesh; human life in   In Christ, Spirit;
       this world, subject to sin   Human life in the new age
       and death and the law,   oriented to God; expressed
       prone to idolatry and vice.   in worship and moral
                                        behaviour.

       incarnation   exaltation

CREATION   PAROUSIA   END (1 Cor. 15.24-28)

C   EMPIRICAL REALITY, that is, Physical world, passing away.

Human existence. On this diagram the central line which
represents the Christ-event reaches the empirical world
where the Son sent by God (8.3) and vindicated by God (1.4;
4.25; 6.4, 9; 8.11, 34; 10.9) was born and was crucified. It
points up to (A) because it is said to be the revelation of
God who is worshipped. This mythic narrative interprets a

historical life and death as God's revelation. It bisects the map of human meanings and values to create contrasting possibilities of human life: believers understand themselves to occupy the new positive possibility, life 'in Christ', in communion with him ('faith'), and Spirit who allots various gifts (12.6-10, cf. 1 Cor. 12). These gifts imply responsibilities; the indicative of Christian existence implies a moral imperative (6.12; 8.12; 12.1–15.13).

Paul's description of the negative alternative form of life is sketched from the perspective of his new self-understanding. The negative accounts of the human condition in 1.18–3.20; 5.12-21 and 7.5-24 are not neutral descriptions but interpretations shaped by their contrast with the new life in Christ. They are not philosophical analyses but form parts of an argument about the nature of Christian existence. Paul's main reason for describing this was probably to imply that Torah observance as a marker of Jewish identity was irrelevant for Gentile believers. In the course of arguing his case he generated symbols which outlived their original intention and gained historic significance (see next chapter).

Christian existence. In all the epistles Paul's pastoral purposes lead him to say most about the positive side of our level 3. He wants to teach Christians what it means to be Christians, and that is why his writings have continued to enlighten later believers. His main rhetorical strategy is to contrast the new with the old and so persuade his hearers to live in their historical world (which includes the empirical level) according to the new life they already share at the level expressed by symbol systems.

The old is described symbolically as 'flesh' on account of humans' natural orientation to their physical needs and desires. The word (*sarx*) can be used neutrally to speak of heredity (1.3; 4.1; 9.3, 5, 8; 11.14) or physicality (2.28), but more typically it represents the human situation as in thrall to sin and consequently headed for death (7.5, 18, 25; 8.3-13; 12.14). In this context the word gathers overtones from self-centred existence (sin) and gets overloaded with negative associations. Coupled with Paul's personal asceticism a door is opened to a gnostic or Manichean denigration of the created order. Paul's aims are quite different. His level 3 contrast between 'flesh' (symbolic) and Spirit sharpens the moral imperatives which he derives from his symbolic description of the reality of Christian existence. This is most clear in Gal. 5.16-25. Reading that epistle is the best preparation for studying Romans. The same contrast between Christian and pre-Christian existence is worked out at length in Romans 5–8. The positive symbols of 5.1-11 are picked up in ch. 8 after the negative reality of human life outside Christ has been symbolized by reference to Adam (5.12-19), sin (6) and the law (7.1-6).

Moral imperatives ('do this!') or prohibitions are drawn from the indicative ('that *is* so') of life in Christ, both within these chapters ('therefore' at 6.12 and 8.12) and on a basis of them. The moral exhortations of chs. 12–15, also beginning with 'therefore' (12.1) follow more naturally from chs. 5–8 than from chs. 9–11. It is because of where believers are (in Christ), empowered by the gift of the Spirit, that human life in accord with God's holy will ensues. Paul's ethical admonitions follow from and are motivated by the character of his symbolic world. This is shaped by Jesus Christ the crucified and risen Lord, the revelation of God whose power is experienced in the present as the Spirit who will also give resurrection life and glory. Paul gives surprisingly little new moral content in his exhortations. He is content to echo synagogue preaching and popular philosophy. He assumes his hearers know what is in accord with God's will and will do it without the support of a codified moral system. All he should need to do is to remind them of their Lord and the Spirit, their present possession and their future hope, but if necessary he will remind them of God's judgment and its moral criterion (2.5-11, cf. 1 Cor. 3.13-14).

Conversion
If level 3 on our symbolic map is Paul's main concern in his epistles to believers (his missionary preaching must have contained more levels 1 and 2 material), and if his moral rhetoric is largely based on contrasting the two possibilities on level 3, we can expect him in moral contexts also to say something about the transition that he and his hearers have

made from the negative reality to the positive reality and possibility. This is described in Rom. 6.2-11, particularly by reference to baptism (vv. 3-5).

The passage is not easy to decode but illustrates what we meant by speaking of Paul's 'symbolic realism'. His language is reminiscent of the mystery religions whose rituals identified initiates with their god. That is not envisaged here, but Paul too is convinced of the reality conveyed by the symbol. Such thinking is not easily grasped by a modern reader. We almost inevitably weaken his language to mere illustrations and dismiss a passage like 1 Cor. 11.30 as superstition or witchcraft. But for Paul (and many today) the religious is more real than the everyday world. The believer has truly passed into the new age, though without physically leaving the old. Believers' lives should therefore express their new orientation to God in Christ. They have broken with the powers that dominated their previous life and the radical character of this break can best be described in terms of dying. This is metaphorical, not literal, language and its force depends on the symbolic realm being no less real than the physical, and disclosing the spiritual which outlasts the material (cf. 2 Cor. 4.18).

The language of death and dying corresponds (anti-thetically) to the usual Jewish and early Christian word for salvation: life. The believer has not yet followed Jesus into the full reality of resurrection life, but has already entered the realm where the power of his resurrection and the Spirit are operative.

Baptism

In the ritual of baptism the believer re-enacts symbolically the death, burial and rising of the Lord, and is somehow united with him. The relationship is described at 6.3-5 by the preposition 'into', by compound verbs using 'with' (*syn-*), by the language of analogy (just as, likeness), and by an organic metaphor (planted). Elsewhere it is called faith, or being 'in Christ', but that refers to its persistence through time. Here Paul needs to sharpen the contrast to the old life by high-lighting the moment of transition. He does not refer to any dramatic subjective experience (such as his own), but to the truth of God made visible in the symbolic act of baptism.

He does not describe baptism sociologically or ecclesiologically by saying anything about the church, even though it *is* the rite of initiation, establishing membership of an earthly community of Jews and Gentiles which he believes is God's eschatological congregation of 'saints'. Instead he describes it christologically, in terms of believers' new relationship with Christ. The church must be presupposed, despite the absence of the word *ecclesia* from Romans 1–15 (it occurs five times in ch. 16 referring to local or house churches), but Christian identity is defined by reference to the crucified and risen Lord, not by one's membership of the ambiguous earthly institution or even the eschatological congregation which Paul does not yet distinguish from this. To be a Christian is to be in Christ, and the meaning of this phrase is defined by its context in Paul's theology as a whole.

These contours of Paul's symbolic world provide a framework in which his peculiar language can be located without attempting a full inventory of his vocabulary and the ways it functions. Some further attention to the central thrust of his religious thought will serve to confirm the fit between our framework and the text of Romans.

Paul's symbolic world hinges on the contrast between the two worlds or 'ages' of Jewish eschatology, this present evil age (Gal. 1.4) and that 'age to come' which he is convinced has already dawned in the resurrection of Christ. The pivotal event of Christ's death and resurrection is thus understood as an eschatological event, the beginning of the end of the old, and the dawn of the new. Paul 'reckoned' himself and his readers to be 'living to God in or through Christ Jesus' (6.11), inhabiting the new, acknowledging Jesus as Lord in a relationship more intimate than that metaphor conveys, and pressing forward to the day when the trials and tribulations of the present will be finally overcome. The central category of Paul's religion, structured by the beliefs and practices of his symbol system, is thus salvation, which means both present transformation and future hope, the truth about human nature and destiny.

This blanket word itself (*sōtēria*), and the related verb 'to

save' (*sōzein*—which also means 'to heal') are generally
reserved by Paul for the future completion of God's plan for
humanity (e.g. 13.11; 5.9-10). They usually refer to the whole
work of God—past, present and future—in mending a dislocated humanity, rather than the partial realization of this in
the historical past of Jesus' death and resurrection and the
existential present of believers. The perfect tense at Eph. 2.5
and 8 is not quite Pauline, and the present participles and
indicative at 1 Cor. 1.18; 15.2; and 2 Cor. 2.15, get their force
from the future they anticipate. The appellation of the
present time as day of salvation at 2 Cor. 6.2 echoes the
Isaiah quotation. But granted that caveat about Paul's
limited use of the actual word, 'salvation' is the overarching
category for what he is constantly talking about: what God in
Christ has done, is doing and will do; and human reception of
and holding fast to that gift or grace. He has little to say
about the mechanics of the salvation event itself, apart from
his echoes of the sacrificial and atonement language of other
Jewish Christians (3.25; 5.9; 8.3) but he uses a variety of
metaphors to describe the contrast between unredeemed and
redeemed existence.

Salvation
The hope of God's ultimate victory over sin and evil in the
world was familiar to Paul from his religious tradition. A
visionary himself (2 Cor. 12), he can use the language of
apocalypse to interpret present suffering and express the
certainty of his hope (8.18-25). The focus of his concern is
humanity's relationship to the Creator, but since humanity is
part of the material world (our level C) his vision embraces
the whole created order. The language of cosmological myth
is inescapable here and this is misinterpreted if Paul's
undoubted concentration on the human world is reduced to
an account of individual human existence that underesti-
mates our interaction with one another and our solidarity
with the natural world. 'Body' (8.23) is multivalent in Paul,
but its reference to human identity includes communication
and the physical.

God is the Creator of all. Nevertheless it is to humans that
the gospel is addressed and the gracious gift of life is offered.
And humans' response to Paul's message is always an indi-

vidual response. Having faith is something no-one can do for you, and in the baptismal confession a person expresses and takes responsibility for his or her personal commitment. Paul sometimes speaks of humanity in corporate terms, those outside Christ (1.18–3.20; 5.12-19) and those inside (5.19; 8) as well as the familiar groupings of Jews and Gentiles. But there is a powerful individualizing aspect to his religion which through Augustine and Luther was to prove hugely influential in Western Christianity and culture. Attention to the symbols which Paul has made common coin should not overshadow the existential reality of faith which this epistle above all has made central in Christianity. 'Faith' is as elusive a term as its correlates 'God' and 'revelation'. Whatever the power of his own religious experience or Christ-mysticism, Paul does not make experience a prerequisite of being in Christ. And yet that loyal and loving attachment to Christ signalled by the word 'faith' is the sum and substance of the new relationship to God, the new age, 'new creation' (2 Cor. 5.17; Gal. 6.15).

Humanity's right relationship to the Creator has been dislocated by Adam's transgression—whether Paul understood that symbol ('Adam' = man) to refer to a historical figure and event or not (we cannot be sure and it does not matter). Through Adam's sin came death (5.12), which Paul can personify as a power like sin and regard as an enemy (1 Cor. 15.26). The physical death inseparable from physical life symbolizes an even more fearful separation from the love of God (cf. 8.35). But as 'through a man (came) death, also through a man resurrection of the dead' (1 Cor. 15.21, cf. Rom. 5.17). Believers shall reign through him (v.17b). That future hope and goal of salvation is for Paul a certainty on account of what has already happened with the dawn of the new age constituted by 'our Lord Jesus Christ', entered by faith in him, and epitomized in Romans by the keyword righteousness (33 times in this epistle; only 14 times elsewhere in Paul).

This theologically and ethically loaded word from Paul's Scripture embraces both the divine initiative, its content, and its result. The forensic background of the word has receded and is barely visible in his use of the noun (it is stronger in his use of the verb, as it is in Second Isaiah). When Paul speaks of God's righteousness and of human righteousness he is speaking of the salvation established in Christ and now to be attained by Jews and Gentiles on the same basis. A related word stressing the divine initiative is 'grace' (24 times in Romans), and one stressing the consequences for humanity is 'peace' (10 times in Romans), the scriptural *shalom* which describes the ideal of the human condition in its relationships.

We have seen how Paul chooses 'right' words (*dik-*) in Romans as part of a scriptural argument found also in Galatians, and also to evoke the Psalter and celebrate God's inclusion of Gentiles (above pp. 18-38). The explosion of judicial metaphors in Western theology and devotion has less support in Paul's intentions than is usually thought. It was natural in the Latin world but was fuelled by and fuelled readings of Romans which Paul would scarcely have acknowledged. He took God's role as judge for granted, however, and the forensic background of the metaphor has not disappeared when it is reapplied to describe the transition from alienation (5.10) to a right relationship with God. It is possible to translate the 'righting' verb (15 times in Romans) 'acquit'—but this is misleading (except at 2.13 and 3.20) because it wrongly suggests the person set free from the court is innocent. But that is not Paul's belief. God liberates sinners, and Paul's emphasis falls on the freedom, not the law-court, on the believer's new relationship to God in the present rather than the forensic background of the metaphor.

Only at 2.13, which is untypical of Paul's soteriological statements (see p. 25) does the adjective 'righteous' (7 times in Romans) speak of human deliverance in a clearly forensic way, and when Paul speaks of freedom elsewhere the law courts are not in view. Western theology has connected Paul's 'right' language with the experience of sin, guilt and forgiveness, but this has little support in the text outside 4.1-9, and even there Paul's intention was rather different (see p. 33). Romans 7 speaks of being enslaved to sin under the law and seems to speak of the experience of impotence if not guilt, but it contains no 'right' language at all. That exegetical observation is not intended to criticize later doctrinal developments—only to insist that they are developments.

More true to Paul's deepest intentions in speaking of what has already happened through Christ's death is the metaphor of reconciling and reconciliation (including peace and love), even though only the verb is found in Romans, and only at 5.10 (both noun and verb occur at 2 Cor. 5.18-20). The idea itself is strongly present also at 5.1-11 and 8.31-39. This metaphor from human relations (cf. 1 Cor. 7.11) is surely the most appropriate when Paul is thinking in terms of individuals' relationship to God (who is personal). He applies it also to God's relationship to the world (2 Cor. 5.19), corresponding to 'new creation' or creature in v.17, but in both verses it is the human world he has in mind. The word reconciliation itself is rare, but the new relationship between God and humans that it expresses is also presupposed in more common terms, such as faith, hope and love.

Where Paul writes of freedom or being liberated (6.18, 20, 22; 7.3; 8.2, 21) the human situation is being seen as slavery. He uses the metaphor of redemption (3.24; 8.23), or being bought out of slavery, to describe both the Christian's present status, arising out of the salvation event in Christ (3.24), and the glorious future still expected (8.21, 23).

The tension between the present and the imminently expected future runs right through Paul's religious experience, his theology and his moral instruction. Christians live 'between the times', as is often pointed out, but also (we may say) in two places. They are citizens of heaven (Phil. 3.21), but colonizing an earth that is passing away. That is because God's new age has dawned in a way that is as yet accessible (5.2) only by faith. The physical world is not yet transformed (8.19-22) but still subject to cosmic powers (8.38-39). Believers are already being transformed and have already been liberated from the powers that held them. Their freedom under the Lord is the truth about themselves. It contrasts with their previous orientation, but creates a tension not yet resolved within a world that continues in its old slavery.

Paul's utopianism is grounded in his present experience of

life lived 'by faith in the Son of God who loved me and gave himself for me' (Gal. 2.20b). His hope of glory involves no denials of present sufferings. He interprets these as sharing in the cross prior to future participation in the Lord's resurrection. The tensions that believers experience between present earthly reality and future hopes, that are no less real, correspond to the contradictions of acknowledging God and so inhabiting God's new world while still confined to the barracks of an older order that is defeated but still has power to exercise its downward pull.

Paul's theological argument against circumcision of Gentile converts is only hinted at in Romans but clearer in Galatians 3–4. It depends on implicitly assigning the law to the powers that believers are freed from (7.4). That seems to go too far (7.7). The law remains God's law (cf. 7.12, 14) and its just requirement is to be met (8.4). But the motivation for the new obedience to God's will is no longer the terms of the Mosaic covenant. It is the fact of inhabiting God's new world that fuels the new obedience. This is where believers are, not under sin but under grace—as Paul should have said at 6.14. His Freudian slip in that verse reveals the undercurrents of his thinking.

How believers less passionate than Paul—or less strongly grounded in a moral tradition—actually behave raises questions about the efficacy of the system. A morality that depends on the persuasive power of religious symbols is only as strong as that symbolic world, and symbol systems are subject to erosion. Paul retained the sanctions of his previous system and reinforced his moral appeals with the popular philosophy and common sense of his day. Christian moral argument has always drawn on many sources. It is above all in the realm of motivation that the symbols function, whether this is by their own allure and/or whether they are vehicles of a transcendent power, the Spirit of God. Our task is not to answer that question of religious truth, but to outline the system and see how it works. Morality is a large part of Paul's religious language and the fact that he was criticized on this front (3.8), perhaps on account of his policy over Torah observance (see pp. 64, 71-72), led him to expose the pattern of his thinking.

This has already been analysed by emphasizing its presuppositions in the already existing religious systems of Judaism and by clarifying their basic shape. Both before and after his call to be an apostle and to Gentile mission, Paul worshipped God the Creator whose self-revelations created the Jewish community and generated the symbols by which that religious community lived. Faith in Christ, the conviction that in Christ God was reconciling the wider world, relativized the Mosaic covenant and impelled Paul to redraw his map of symbols and justify his new missionary practice. But the symbolic materials he used remained those available in his tradition or (subject to their suitability) in the world of his hearers.

The metaphors already considered contrast the old and new status through terms drawn from human social interaction in its institutions of slavery and the law courts. Paul can also illuminate this by other metaphors, drawn from the natural world which God created. These speak of transformation, or life in contrast to death. They appear most clearly in 1 Corinthians 15 and 2 Corinthians 3–5, but are also present in the contrast between Adam and Christ in Romans 5, in the interpretation of baptism in 6.3-5 and in the hope of glory in ch. 8. This 'change of form' into the image of the risen Christ means life instead of death, and union with Christ. All such language belongs on level 3 in our diagram. It contrasts the old existence prior to Christ and the new sphere which is entered by the ritual re-enactment of Christ's death and resurrection in baptism. The contrast itself works rhetorically to persuade readers to identify with the new. In the new life in Christ, gifted with the Spirit, the finitude and failure of the old Adam are overcome. Human longing that the inevitability of decay and physical dissolution may not be the last word about humanity is met by talk of the Risen One and a conviction of some present association with him.

That is all articulated by what is said about Jesus as well as through the symbolism relating to salvation. One major point at which Paul's talk of salvation coincides with what he has to say about Jesus is in his sacrificial interpretation of his death (above p. 100). The importance of this language for Paul himself is uncertain on account of his probable use of

earlier traditions (above p. 90). He accepted and used these,
but they may have been less vital to him than to some of his
first-century and subsequent readers.

This sacrificial language should not be isolated from the
rest of Paul's soteriological language, nor should Paul's array
of images be seen as different elements of a theological
system. He connects sacrificial ideas with his 'righting'
language at 5.9 (and obscurely at 2 Cor. 5.21), and the explanation ('for') of 'righted' in terms of having been reconciled to
God through the death of God's Son (v.10) shows that he
could mix his symbolism without specifying different steps in
a process. Later doctrinal thinking is more precise, and the
way Paul has been quarried makes the task of understanding exactly what he was saying and doing more
difficult. One reason for being aware of those later doctrinal
developments (ch. 6) is to be free from their unconscious
influence. That Paul's symbols lent themselves to doctrinal
development is evidence of their power, but historians and
exegetes want to see him in his first-century context. Our
study of his symbolic world is intended to assist that, as well
as to facilitate a modern theological interpretation.

Some interpreters dismiss sacrificial ideas as a relic of
other cultures (including some that still exist). Like the
Stoics they prefer to reduce sacrifice to a metaphorical,
'rational' sacrifice as Paul does at 12.1. Paul presumably
shared the assumptions of Second Temple Jews about
sacrifice, and clearly echoed earlier Christians' belief that the
death of Jesus was a sacrifice, perhaps seen as purifying
God's people for the new age. But it is the narrative of Jesus
rather than the mechanics of atonement that interests him.
He interprets the history of Jesus theologically, and
sacrificial ideas assist in that, but his fulcrum is the death
and resurrection of Jesus as the eschatological event which
inaugurates the new age to be entered now by faith in Christ.
He usually speaks of the death of Jesus without using
sacrificial terms. When he draws on these ideas they function
to dramatize God's love for all in Jesus (8.32-35; 5.1-11, cf. Jn
15.13), rather than to explain why Jesus died. The death of
Christ is central for Paul as sacrificial ideas are not. It occu-
pies both ends of the central arrow in our diagram. The

second Adam became obedient unto death, and it is as the One crucified for us that he is now raised to be the centre of Paul's Christian symbolic world.

The metaphors drawn from the law courts, the slave-market and human friendship focus attention on the contrast between the human situation before and after God's saving initiative and the proper response to that. The sacrificial idea is prominent because it directs attention to the saving event itself, the ground and prerequisite of Christian proclamation and the response of faith. But its alignment with reconciliation language suggests that its main function is to insist that the death of Jesus was God's doing and an event of self-giving love.

Corporate terms
The death and resurrection of Christ are central for Paul. Nevertheless, the 'revelation event' is ultimately the person, not what happens to him, and not some mythological trans-action in the heavenly realm. The person has become a symbol, making him accessible to believers, not merely a figment of the mythopoetic imagination or an actor in some cosmic drama. Paul does not, therefore, rest content with traditional formulations. It is not simply the death and resurrection but the person whose significance is communi-cated. To this end the crucified and risen Jesus is described not only as an individual, the messiah our Lord, but also in corporate terms. The Christ who is seated at level 2 in our diagram, the crucified Jesus who has been vindicated by God, is like Adam a corporate figure who embraces and embodies the whole collectivity of believers (Rom. 5.12-19).

This is expressed most simply by the phrase 'in Christ' (8.1) whose resonances are not exhausted by the instru-mental interpretation ('by' or 'through Christ'). That refer-ence to the eschatological event itself admittedly predominates, but the properly spatial or 'local' meaning of 'in' is occasionally present (cf. Phil. 3.9 where 'to be found' implies a place). Even though at Rom. 8.1 'in Christ' can be translated weakly as 'Christians', Paul's use of such a rich and pregnant phrase to describe Christian existence shows that for him this is a strong category. Like 'faith' it speaks of a relationship to Christ which mediates a relationship to God.

The 'body of Christ' metaphor at 1 Cor. 12.27 (cf. v. 12) is similar, and the two ideas are combined at Rom. 12.5. Paul does not quite say, as Colossians and Ephesians do, that the church is the body of Christ. Neither is it quite accurate to translate 'in Christ' as 'in the church', whether considered institutionally or even when considered symbolically as the eschatological congregation. All who are in Christ *are* members of the church and became such when they were baptized 'into Christ', but to render the phrase in that way would shift the accent away from Christ himself. It is hard to doubt that Paul has a strong sense of the whole people of God, even though when he uses the word 'church' he is usually referring to local churches. But the cast of his religious thought is christological, not ecclesiological, contrary to the opinion of some recent interpreters.

'Putting on the Lord Jesus Christ' at Rom. 13.14 is another phrase suggestive of the corporate Christ. It may imply a great cosmic shirt enfolding all believers rather than an individual's Van Heusen. At Gal. 3.27 the individual's baptismal robe is evoked, but even there *everyone* who is baptized is said to have put on Christ. This solidarity of believers with Christ, expressed also at 2 Cor. 5.14 ('one died for all, therefore all died') and Gal. 3.28 ('you are all one person in Christ Jesus'), implies that Paul thinks of Christ in corporate as well as individual terms. That is represented in our diagram by 'level 3 positive' (the idea and ideal of Christian community) depending directly on level 2, the revelation person and event of the crucified and risen Lord.

Church
The church itself, whether local or universal, receives surprisingly little symbolic elaboration from Paul, in striking contrast to Ephesians and later New Testament writings which mark the emergence of catholic Christianity. The 'people of God' idea, or God's covenant with God's people, was fundamental to Paul's Jewish religious thinking. It is echoed in the opening of the epistle and drawn on heavily in chs. 9–11 where the point at issue concerns empirical Israel. But it is not even the main point of Paul's discussion of Abraham

as forefather in ch. 4. The emphasis falls more on Abraham's faith than on the community of Jews and Gentiles whose father he in consequence is. The argument that Abraham's right relationship with God depended on faith not 'works' (in effect, ritual) was probably designed to defend the practice of admitting Gentiles as gentiles, without requiring them to be circumcised. It is concerned with social realities and these receive a symbolic tincture from the scriptural argument itself in vv. 11-12. But when Paul is articulating his system of symbols in his own way rather than defending it by scriptural argument he speaks of believing, or being 'in Christ', or belonging to Christ (8.9; 1 Cor. 3.23), or being members of the body that is Christ (1 Cor. 12.12, cf. v. 27), rather than membership of the church. The institution is mythologized as the eschatological congregation, and that is reflected in the words 'saints', 'called', and 'people', but this symbolic reality is always subordinate to christology, as our diagram indicates.

That is not to underestimate the importance of social realities for Paul. He has at 4.11 the historical reality of *all* believers in mind and doubtless takes for granted their membership of the wider body as well as local congregations. One whose whole activity was directed to building up local churches can scarcely be suspected of lacking an ecclesiology. Yet the metaphors for the local church which he uses to motivate his readers' behaviour (e.g. planting, building, and Temple at 1 Cor. 3; body at 1 Cor. 12) do not make the ontological claim of those which make up his symbolic world. They are illustrations rather than symbols which carry human meanings and ground these in the reality of God's intervention. Perhaps because he is constantly thinking about the actual churches he has founded and still guides pastorally (cf. 2 Cor. 11.28), the church belongs more on our level C, empirical reality, than to his symbolic world (B). His writings imply an ecclesiology and provided materials for later ecclesiology but this is not the focus of his own theological reflection. It is more appropriate to Paul's thought to analyse what it means·to be a Christian, in corporate as well as individual terms, than to describe how he thinks of 'the Church'.

The exposition and argument of Romans give little theory about the church, even though the framework of the epistle shows this is Paul's constant concern. Even his insistence that both Jews and Gentiles belong to it, and on the same basis, can scarcely be called a theory, as it can in Ephesians. This argument is conducted by Paul in terms of Scripture (what God has done) and the nature of Christian existence (chs. 5–8) rather than in terms of the nature of the church itself (ecclesiology). Here the main symbols, which for Paul are powerful realities, are the corporate Christ and the Spirit.

Holy Spirit
Paul's understanding of the Spirit provides the clearest link between our three levels of his symbolic world and the empirical world in which Christian faith is lived out in ministry, mutual love, personal integrity, and civil obedience. As in Scripture and Jewish tradition the Spirit is the Spirit or breath of God, God in action, powerful to create or recreate, to change individuals or resurrect them (Ezek. 37, cf. Rom. 1.3) and to renew the face of the earth (Ps. 104). But for Paul the Spirit of God is also the Spirit of Christ (8.9). This is no impersonal force because the God who creates and saves is known in his saving righteousness in the death and resurrection of Jesus who is present to believers as Spirit. The Lord who is Spirit and creates freedom (cf. 2 Cor. 3.14-18) works on earth through believers who are empowered by this Spirit. That gift or grace (*charis*, 12.3) is concreted in particular gifts (*charismata*, 12.6; 1 Cor. 12.4, 31) which are gifts of the Spirit (*pneumatika*, 1 Cor. 12.1). In the general paraenesis of Romans 12–13, 12.6-10 summarizes part of what is said at greater length in 1 Corinthians 12–14.

These passages provided the springboard for Luther's theory of every Christian having a vocation and ministry, and seeing secular employment as instances of this. Paul has the Christian community's worship and pastoral concern in mind, but the principle is the same: the 'Spirit', which we have located in Paul's symbolic world without prejudice to the question of its transcendent reality, is operative in the historical world of Christian and (we may add) other institutions.

Ethics

That principle holds of Pauline ethics in general. Both these passages in Romans and 1 Cointhians. speak of love, which is their heart and centre; the second table of the decalogue can be summarized by the Lev. 19.18 instruction to love they neighbour (Rom. 13.8-10). No one is more eloquent than Paul in speaking of love at 1 Corinthians 13, and it is love of neighbour that he means. Only Rom. 8.28 and 1 Cor. 8.3 speak explicitly of loving God, though the affective dimension of faith is expressed in other terms. But for Paul this love of the neighbour lived out in the empirical world is elicited by way of response to God's love made known to believers in Christ (Gal. 2.20; Rom. 5.5-8), and poured into our hearts through the Holy Spirit that is given us (5.5). In other words it is God's initiative in the gospel which is the source and motivation of Paul's moral suasions. That can only be articulated in terms of Paul's symbolic world, but it implies a power experienced as guiding everyday life.

That is the theory. In practice Paul constantly finds it necessary to reinforce this indicative of Christian existence with moral imperatives. However, the form of these is significant. It is a matter of persuasion: I exhort you (12.1), beseech you, urge you. Only very rarely does Paul appeal to his own authority and demand a particular course of action, as in 1 Corinthians 5. He never does so in Romans, even though he is explicit about his apostolic authority and gift (1.5; 15.15-16). That commission to preach and to teach includes giving moral instruction, but Christian moral instruction points to the gospel of God's love and expects behaviour to follow from the believer's response and new status; it is not a matter of casuistry.

The effect of this structure to Paul's thought is that his most powerful moral appeals are quite general in content. 6.12-14, 8.4-14, and 12.1-2 are remarkably unspecific. Paul could rest with that because he could presuppose a strong moral tradition from his Jewish background, including the teaching of Jesus (12.14, 17). Nowhere does he break with this moral tradition in the light of the gospel, as he breaks with Jewish ritual practice. At times he recycles the moral tradition uncritically, and this makes it inadvisable to treat his epistles as oracles. Paul himself must be read critically, and that will not necessarily mean disagreeing with him. What he says about homosexuality at 1.27 or the state at 13.1-7 echoes older tradition. It has considerable weight and authority, but is not exempt from Paul's general instruction to test (12.2) or try to discern what the will of God is. In matters of political and sexual ethics contemporary Christians are not excused from the hard work of deciding what is right and wrong just because Paul in his day thought certain matters beyond dispute. That is not to devalue Paul's contribution to Christian moral thinking but to avoid devaluing moral thinking itself.

The eschatological sanction for ethics is taken over from Judaism (judgment according to works, 2.5-11) and given Christian emphasis at 13.11-14 by reference to present eschatology and the imminent parousia. Again it is the language of Paul's symbolic world that is intended to motivate Christian behaviour. An example of its impact was given above on p. 109.

The most likely example in Romans of Paul's moral guidance being directed to a particular situation is found in 14.1–15.13. This passage has rightly been sifted for clues as to Paul's purposes in writing (above, pp. 63-65). But regardless of the situation in Rome this section illuminates the religious basis of Paul's moral guidance. His moral thinking is an important aspect of his religious language because morality is an important aspect of religion. Whether it can also stand independently of religion was not an issue for Paul and need not concern us here.

It is probable that 'the strong' and 'the weak in faith' refer to those who can sit light to Jewish eating customs, and those who cannot. That was not merely a matter of avoiding forbidden food, such as pork, but avoiding all meat because it might have been sacrificed to an idol, and wine which might have been offered as a libation. Idolatry rather than food laws was the issue in 1 Corinthians 8 and 10, and possibly in Romans too, though 14.14 rather supports the alternative (*kashrut*) possibility. Similarly at 14.5, 'distinguishing days' presumably refers (tactfully) to Jewish Christian Sabbath observance. Paul can give a positive religious interpretation

of either practice (v. 6). This orientation of both patterns of
life to the Lord, the centre of every Christian believer's
symbol system, has immediate bearing on relations within
the Christian community. A busy interest in, and condemnation of alternative lifestyles is simply inappropriate. We shall
all answer for our own moral decisions (v. 10) and are therefore (Paul implies) already answerable to our own
consciences. But that is not all. Our personal decisions, right
in themselves, might play havoc with others' faith. In a
community we have to avoid scandal. That is not hypocrisy;
it is love.

Paul himself identifies with the 'strong' at 14.14 and 15.1,
but respects the scruples of the weak while not allowing
them to dictate to the strong and abrogate their Christian
freedom. We may waive our freedom. If there seems here a
bias to the weak, that is because they are on the other side
from Paul himself. Christ did not please himself (15.3).
Respect for others takes priority over our own rights, at least
in matters that are ultimately of no importance, such as
cultic preferences (14.17).

Worship
Not that cultic practice is unimportant. Paul's ecumenical
guidance on overcoming these unhappy divisions between
believers is directed towards enabling them to worship
together (15.6). That is to be the expression of true community (v. 5) rooted in what God has done and is doing and
(faith hopes) will do. Even the judgments of the individual
conscience are considered by Paul in a context of universal
worship (14.11), and this whole instruction to accept one
another as Christ accepted you with a view to God's glory
(15.7) reaches its climax in Scripture's celebration of Jews
and Gentiles worshipping God together. This is the
fulfilment of God's promise to the patriarchs (15.8). Even
when Paul has his own Gentile mission in mind he never
loses sight of its Jewish roots. The Gentiles' hope is in the
scion of Jesse and this evokes a doxology to the God of hope
who fills worshippers with all joy and peace in believing, so
that they may abound in hope through the power of Holy
Spirit (15.13).

The goal of Christian life in the present is thus to be directed towards God, and this finds expression in worshipping together. Paul can use cultic language to describe his own efforts towards the Gentiles achieving this goal (15.16). In terms of our model, worship is the time believers are explicit about their symbolic world, attending to God by articulating the symbols which direct them to the reality of God. It is an end in itself and needs no justification beyond the truth of God and the authenticity of the revelation by which God is known. But it has the side-effect of keeping the worshipper's symbol system in good repair and able to be a medium through which God's power of Spirit directs or inspires everyday life.

Worship and Christian ethics are thus closely intertwined, and Paul can speak not only of his own apostolic activity (15.16) but of all Christian life (12.1-2) in terms of sacrifice, that is, worship. He entreats his Christian readers to 'offer and present unto thee, O Lord, ourselves, our souls and bodies, to be a reasonable holy and lively sacrifice unto thee,' as a later rite inspired by St. Augustine was to paraphrase his words. In 6.19 and 22 (cf. 1 Thess 4.3, 4, 7; 1 Cor. 1.30) the cultic word traditionally translated sanctification (hagiasmos) means consecration, that is, a life dedicated, set apart for God, like the word *hagioi* for Christians: saints, set apart for God (1.7 etc.).

If Christian conduct is ultimately self-dedication to God the language of worship is the best way to sum it up. But the Christian life is also life in community, and the texture of Paul's instruction is nowhere clearer than when he seeks to remove barriers to Christian community. Here and in 1 Corinthians we see robust common sense, clarity on principles (14.14), flexibility in practice, gentleness in application. Constant reference is made to the Lord because the ideas and ideals of Christian community (level 3) flow from the revelation event itself and are coloured by the character of that event (15.3).

That these symbols find practical realization in the personal and corporate life of all believers in Rome the apostle can only entreat and pray. His epistle begins (1.8-10) and ends (15.13, 30-33) in prayer, and it is in prayer that the

Spirit finds expression at a climactic point of the exposition (8.16, 26-27). The undertone of prayer is also present in the frequent quotation of and allusion to the Psalter. Paul's language in Romans includes celebration, argument, instruction, confession and doxology, but what makes it all *religious* language is its proximity to prayer, because that is where faith is explicit. On the other hand language is not life itself. It is in personal relationships, and the institutions that support them, that faith finds its many forms. That is why moral exhortation is prominent, and love its central category. The scriptural argument in chs. 1–4, and the appeal to Christian experience in chs. 5–8 are subservient to that in the sense that they tell what makes authentic human existence and true community possible. That is what Paul calls good news from God, the saving event of Jesus Messiah, which it is his joy and privilege to communicate.

6

THE IMPACT
OF ROMANS

THE CULTURAL IMPORTANCE and interest of a religious text lie
as much if not more in what others have made of it as in
what the author intended. Paul's greatest epistle has had an
incalculable effect on the development of Christianity and so
on European and American history, regardless of how
correctly he has been understood. Lines taken out of context
have swayed opinion by their rhetorical power. The incorpo-
ration of Romans into Christian Scripture and its use in
lectionaries and preaching have encouraged closer attention
to short passages than to the sweep of Paul's argument.

That has proved less misleading than it might, on account
of the correspondences between the original context and that
of most Christian interpreters. Both Paul and the majority of
his readers were (and still are) concerned to understand
what Christianity essentially *is* or should be, and what moral
consequences follow. Paul may have had a negative consequence in mind, that male Gentile converts need not be
circumcised, but he wrapped this up in a positive statement
and argument about what Christianity essentially is, and
this has continued to reverberate. The main problem Paul
faced in the 50s has not been an issue for any except his
earliest readers, but Paul sets his negative response in the
context of a generally positive statement of the gospel. Even
Galatians, which addresses the circumcision problem more
directly, has proved helpful to Christians not affected by the
issue that occasioned it.

Most Christian readers have agreed with what Karl Barth in his 1921 Preface to *The Epistle to the Romans* called his 'primary assumption': that 'Paul knows of God what most of us do not know; and his epistles enable us to know what he knew' (p. 11). That is a bold pair of assumptions. Our preceding chapters have neither denied nor confirmed them, but they have tried to avoid ignoring—and so implicitly denying—the religious claims which Paul makes in this text. Whether these are true can be decided only in the conscience of individual readers. The aim of theological interpreters is to help make that decision possible by aiding understanding of what Paul wrote, and doing so in a way that does not obscure what he meant. One-sided attention to other, non-theological matters raised by the text can be a way of obscuring Paul's primary concern.

Exactly how 'his epistles (might) enable us to know what he knew' is less simple than Barth's simple remark might imply. Coming to a knowledge of God involves more than reading the epistles, because more than communication of information is involved. This has its place. Information from the religious tradition is an essential vehicle and ingredient. But neither knowing God nor even understanding Paul can be reduced to knowing the tradition. Knowing God (in Paul's opinion) involves the 'obedience of faith'; understanding Paul must therefore include some appreciation of what that is and how he aims to elicit it. Interpreters of Paul who respect his intentions without sharing them need to be sensitive to the logic of his religious discourse. Those who share his religious commitment and hope to communicate something of the apostle's religious insight are engaged on an even more delicate task. Their hope must be that the subject matter will somehow come to speak for itself if some of the barriers to understanding can be overcome.

These barriers are only partly linguistic. Paul's Greek teems with exegetical ambiguities, constantly forcing translators to choose one interpretation or another. Their choices depend less often on grammar and syntax than on their assessment of Paul's whole theology and purpose. Historical and literary judgment are therefore as necessary as linguistic competence, and religious sensitivity as important as either.

These necessary skills and tasks can be distinguished by an analogy. Historical and exegetical techniques serve as a telescopic lens to reconnoitre the far side of the gulf that separates us from an ancient culture refracted in a text. But historical understanding of a religion demands more than this. It requires us imaginatively to 'go' there and breathe its air. We may still remain observers rather than full participants, but observing from a distance by telescope is not enough. Mentally to cross over and feel the ground requires conceptual bridges such as those built in the scientific study of religion. These draw on a wide range of religious data, including some interpreters' own experience. They illuminate the material and may help some to understand their own position in relation to the world of the text. At least they establish enough points of contact to secure a footbridge between that world and our own.

Most of Paul's interpreters have wanted both less and more than historical understanding of the ancient world. They have not wanted to be ancient historians, but to occupy the territory over the gulf and make it their own. Stronger bridges are needed to carry the constant flow of religious traffic involved in using this ancient text as part of one's own Scripture. The Christian doctrinal tradition has functioned in this way so successfully that many readers of Romans today hear more of that tradition than of the apostle himself.

Biblical scholarship has usually seen that as a failure to be remedied. It sees its prime responsibility to the world of the text itself. But there is more to be said, both about the text itself and about the cultural and educational responsibilities of the scholars.

The Russian literary critic Bakhtin explains how great works 'continue to live in the distant future. In the process of their posthumous life they are enriched with new meanings, new significance: it is as though these works outgrow what they were in the epoch of their creation' (*Speech Genres and Other Essays*, p. 4). He illustrates this by 'that "great Shakespeare" whom we know now', and denies any possibility of 'squeezing our Shakespeare into the Elizabethan epoch'. He asks, 'Do we then attribute to Shakespeare's works something that was not there, do we modernize and distort them?'. While recognizing that possibility he insists that Shakespeare 'has grown because of that which actually has been and continues to be found in his works, but which neither he himself nor his contemporaries could consciously perceive and evaluate in the context of the culture of their epoch' (p. 4).

Bakhtin's theory that 'semantic phenomena can exist in concealed form, potentially, and be revealed only in semantic cultural contexts of subsequent epochs that are favourable for such disclosure' (p. 5) provides a model to explain aspects of what a religion finds in its scripture. Those who agree with him that 'the semantic treasures of Shakespeare embedded in his works were created and collected through the centuries and even millennia' will have no difficulty in saying that of the Bible too. If they agree with him that 'these could not be fully revealed or recognized in his epoch' they have here a theory of inspiration relating Scripture and subsequent tradition. But regardless of theological theories they will surely join in calling for a biblical scholarship which traces not only the pre-history of an author's motifs, and the history of his or her situation, aims and audience, but also traces their posthumous life in the history of their reception by subsequent readers.

The preceding chapters of this book have respected the conventions of modern biblical scholarship and given most prominence to the historical question of what Paul meant, while hinting that this is less separable from the hermeneutical question of what the text means for a contemporary reader than is usually admitted. It is after all a contemporary reader who is trying to understand and express what Paul meant. But the historical conscience is important for anyone who agrees with Barth that Paul knew something of God. Much as our own subjectivity is involved in learning from his epistles something of what he knew, the kind of objectivity for which historians strive provides a check against simply reading into the text our own religious opinions. Barth anticipated modern literary theory by recognizing that no-one can bring out the meaning of a text without at the same time adding something to it, and he admitted the danger of adding more than we extract (p. ix). His admirers among biblical scholars have taken the point and given more weight to the historical perspective. But Barth's concern with the *Sache*, the theological subject matter, or what Paul thought he was writing about, remains to point a finger at theologians whose historical enthusiasms have pushed theological interests into the shade.

One major commentary series, the ecumenical *Evangelisch-Katholischer Kommentar*, has in principle, if not always in practice, acknowledged the role that the history of interpretation can play in opening up the theological dimensions of the biblical texts. The role is both negative and positive, and its value is not restricted to theologians. Most readers come to this text with some conceptual baggage inherited from earlier interpreters, along with their other cultural assumptions. Believers have internalized detailed maps of the biblical territory that they want to occupy, and most other students have read or picked up something from the memoirs of those who have visited it before them. But these are mostly written in outmoded languages and are sometimes no doubt inaccurate. The negative function of knowing about earlier interpretations is to help free us from them. We prefer our modern equipment, the telescopic lens of historical and exegetical method.

The knowledge which these methods provide, however, is limited in scope, and less than some readers are wanting. The positive aspect of the history of interpretation is the possibility that those older explorers also knew something worth knowing, and may help us to hear what Paul was intending, and may suggest ways of taking the conversation further.

There can be no question of choosing between attending to the history of interpretation and making our own exegetical judgments. We have to sort out the baggage received from the past, and historical exegesis remains an essential criterion. But there is a case for pursuing it in tandem with some reflection on the 'posthumous life' of the text being studied. Even a brief sketch of such a large topic may prove suggestive.

The impact of this epistle on believers in Rome (and possibly elsewhere) in the 50s is not clear, but it was preserved, and presumably read, because it was familiar a generation later to Clement of Rome, and perhaps to the (probably Roman) author of 1 Peter. It probably influenced the writer of Ephesians and (more speculatively) may have been known to the author of Luke–Acts, again perhaps in Rome at the end of the century. It perhaps influenced Luke's conception: to the Jew first, then to the Greek. And Acts 13.38-39 looks like a literary echo of Romans, especially if (as suggested above) Paul's 'right' language was specific to a particular argument rather than being the usual language of his missionary preaching. Jas 2.14-26 is probably trying to correct what the author (or others) wrongly thought Romans was saying. It would be possible to construct a theory about the origins of the New Testament in which our epistle was the nucleus: the collection of Paul's letters perhaps in the 90s (by 'Luke'?) may have stimulated others too, including the (possibly Roman) author of Hebrews. But the evidence here is not conclusive; proposals are based largely on guesswork.

The ground is a little more solid in the second century, and here Rome is already a major Christian centre. We cannot suppose Pliny and Trajan, or even Josephus or Epictetus, ever heard of Paul or his epistle, and if Flavius Clemens did before his execution by Domitian in 95 and Domitilla did before her banishment they have left no record. But the major Christian writers of the time—Clement, Hermas, Ignatius, Polycarp, Valentinus, Marcion, Justin, Tatian, and Irenaeus—all visited or lived in Rome. The capital became significant for the emergence of early catholicism and the rejection of heresy. The martyrdom of Peter and Paul there was part of Rome's appeal, and even though some (like Justin) distrusted Paul's epistles on account of their usefulness to the Christian gnostics and Marcion, it is hard to doubt that our epistle contributed to Rome's prestige. Paul was for Gentile Christians 'the apostle' par excellence, and by the time of Irenaeus (c. 180) his epistles had become a virtually scriptural source for Christian theological vocabulary.

In some ways Marcion was more Pauline than the orthodox, despite his cutting Jesus and Paul loose from their

Jewish roots and from the God of Israel, the Creator. We shall return to the aspect of Paul's influence adumbrated by Marcion and assess its true value later, but that was not the point at which Paul shaped early Christian history. The full impact of Paul's letters on Christianity owed more to his learned and enthusiastic admirers in Alexandria, the seedbed of patristic theology and exegesis.

Clement and Origen interpreted Paul within the framework of their Christian Platonism, minimizing his ambivalence about the Jewish law and understanding his teaching on predestination (Rom. 9) as divine foreknowledge. Origen's commentary (c. 247), exercised a huge influence over subsequent writers East and West. In his exegesis of Romans 5 he moved away from his earlier speculation on the fall and closer to later Western debate on original sin, but in general his Paul is the spiritual man rather than the justified sinner, and he owes more to Romans 8 than to chs. 5–7. He sees that 3.28 implies 'faith alone', but does not see this as antithetical to moral or religious practice. Origen was not a Lutheran.

Eastern theologians concerned with the doctrine of God and the person of Christ saw little of what the West was to find in Romans. They discussed christological texts, especially Rom. 1.3; 8.3, and 9.5, but showed little interest in Paul's major themes.

Fragments of commentaries from Alexandria (Cyril) and the Antiochenes (Diodore, Theodore, Theodoret) survive in the medieval *Catenae* (chains of quotation) but most are lost. This rich exegetical tradition supported the constant reading of Romans in the liturgy, and in expository preaching as best represented by Chrysostom's 32 Homilies (c. 390; English, 3rd edn, 1877). These remind us that the direct impact of Paul on the pew has always been moral and ascetical rather than theological. Lists of vices are more intelligible than Paul's arguments. Chrysostom's Homily 4 attacks homosexual practices (not homoerotic love) as unnatural. Thus has Rom. 1.26-27 echoed through Christian history from Clement *(Paidagogos* 2.10) to the present day.

Teaching not central to the theme or argument of the epistle inevitably gained disproportionate influence when it addressed an important topic. Rom. 13.1-7 is arguably the most historically influential paragraph Paul ever wrote. In Homily 23 Chrysostom made a contribution to political theory by discussing it, as did later medieval theologians. Against John of Salisbury *(Policraticus* 8) and St Thomas *(ST II*, 2, 42, art. 2), the Council of Constance (1415) decided these verses forbade tyrannicide. Verses 3-4 were often combined with Lk. 22.38-39 (the two swords) to justify the medieval church's exercising political power. Much later the great importance of Romans 13 for socially conservative Lutherans impeded resistance to Hitler.

Western reception of Romans in general has made this epistle (together with Isaiah, Matthew and John) one of the main pillars of Christian Scripture. Tertullian and Cyprian in Africa and Hippolytus in Rome quoted it as Scripture but were scarcely influenced by its theology. 'Ambrosiaster' (as Erasmus named him) was perhaps a converted Jew. His practical historical sense and his understanding of Judaism led to a commentary (c. 365–80) which is unmatched in anticipating modern scholarship. It influenced the (recently republished) expositions of Pelagius which were widely read in the belief they had been written by St Jerome, and it was also studied by Augustine who quoted its comment on Rom. 5.12 that everyone sinned in Adam. The Old Latin rendering *(in quo)* which suggested this mistaken exegesis continued to guide both Catholic and Protestant theology long after being challenged by Erasmus in 1516. The exegesis is wrong, but the doctrine of original sin may still appeal to v. 19.

Combined with the Genesis story of creation and the fall, Rom. 5.12-21 has had a huge influence on Christian thought and has been used to justify the baptism of infants. The doctrine of original sin is part of a wider complex of ideas which are fundamental to many religions: their assessment of the human condition, or anthropology. This must correspond to ideas about how the human predicament is put right or remedied, that is, 'salvation'.

Paul's elaboration of both anthropology and soteriology (level 3 negative and positive in the previous chapter) earned Romans its central role in Christian thinking. But it was only in the West and starting with Augustine that the

Christian faith was expounded largely in terms of the human subject in contrast to Eastern preoccupation with the doctrine of God and christology. So it was with Augustine (who also improved on Eastern trinitarian doctrine) that Romans 3–7 became a vital source of Christian theology. The earlier treatise on anthropology by Nemesius of Emesa in Syria had been based on Plato not Paul. The Alexandrine Didymus the Blind had discussed Romans 7 in his work *Against the Manichaeans*, but it was the former Manichaean sympathizer from Hippo who made these chapters central for both theology and philosophy.

The interaction in the Pelagian controversy of Augustine's personal experience, biblical study, liturgical practice, church politics and even imperial authority, warns against any simple model of the relationship between exegesis and theology. But the steadily increasing impact of his study of Romans had historic consequences. His theory of original guilt did not become Christian orthodoxy and neither did his hard line on predestination, but his discussions set the medieval agenda, found some supporters, and were developed in the Augustinian revival of the early sixteenth century commonly called the Reformation.

The germ of all this may be found in 396, when Simplicianus's perplexity about God hating Esau (9.13) led Augustine to a longer treatment of Rom. 9.10-29 than he had provided in his short anti-Manichaean exposition of the epistle in 394. He now accepted that election precedes justification and by relating these doctrinal themes systematically (in a way that Paul does not) he made predestination a problem for Christian doctrine. When Pelagius later protested against Augustine's doctrine of grace, predestination increasingly provided its bulwark, at whatever dreadful cost to human freedom. That story continued with Calvin and provided an ideological engine driving English, Scottish and American puritanism to capitalism and economic domination of the world.

It was not the real Paul, and not the best of Augustine. More immediately influential on medieval Catholicism and its Reformation revival and development was Augustine's related use of Paul's 'righteousness', 'right', and 'righting' terminology in Romans, or (as it became through its even more forensic flavour in Latin): justice (divine and human) and justification, or making just (*iustitia, iustificatio, iustificare*).

This Latin legal frame of reference for the relationship of God to humanity has a very different flavour from Paul's conviction about God's faithfulness to the covenant. As Catholic priests Augustine and Luther read Paul alongside the Psalter and caught more of his heart's religion than many theologians and jurists over the eleven centuries between them, but this Western reception of Paul's forensic language in Romans generated a powerful misreading. To understand this it is necessary to jump seven centuries beyond Augustine into the doctrine of the atonement.

The legal flavour of the Latin phrase *iustitia Dei* (justice of God) was always recognized. The father of Latin theology, Tertullian, was a lawyer. But the question of its relationship to God's mercy became urgent when Anselm of Canterbury shifted discussion of human salvation from mythological into moral and legal categories. *Proslogion* 9 understands God's justice to include God's mercy. This attempt to root God's saving act (justifying grace) in philosophical reflection on God's nature is foreign to Paul, but not contrary to his unstated assumptions, and Anselm is here broadly true to the main thrust of what Paul says of God and salvation in Romans.

The point at which Anselm's theory took Christian theology away from Paul was in his idea of 'satisfaction' or payment of a debt to God for the injury done to God's honour by human sin. These categories made sense in Anselm's feudal society and built upon the long established doctrine of Christ's divinity. Only the perfect Son of God could, by his wholly innocent death, pay the debt incurred by humanity. That is 'why God became man' (*Cur Deus homo*). This could easily suggest an unjust Father demanding the death of his innocent Son in order to satisfy his honour or the abstract demands of his justice. It creates a tension between God's justice and God's mercy. The sacrificial language of Rom. 3.25b could be read in this way, but Paul is clear (3.25a; 5.8) that the whole event stems from God's loving initiative.

Anselm's theory expresses important aspects of Christian belief, but its weaknesses became more apparent as justification, understood in strongly forensic terms, became the central theme in protestant theology and was more systematically connected with sacrificial ideas than Paul's abbreviated comments at 5.9 and 2 Cor. 5.21 had implied. This led to ideas of atonement which were rejected most fiercely in the Enlightenment and are still as hateful to liberals as they are attractive to Calvinists and other evangelicals. Paul refers to 'blood' at 3.25 and 5.9 (and in the eucharistic passages 1 Cor. 10.16; 11.27, 29). Colossians and Ephesians develop his language, but those who change 'saved by his precious blood' to 'love' in Mrs Alexander's hymn are also true to Paul, and right to relativise his sacrificial language (as above p. 118).

This whole theme of atonement has stimulated some of the most profound probing of the human situation in Christian theology. The main source of its appeal lies in the solution it offers to the problem of guilt. The 'introspective conscience of the West' (Stendahl, see p. 151) was given its initial impulse by St Augustine and developed in Western monasticism and penitential discipline. It flowered in pietism and the residue of that is still found in Christian hymn books. The psychological and theological value of this development is not to be underestimated, but it has moved a long way from its Pauline roots.

An example of the importance of Romans for medieval theology is Abelard developing an alternative theory of the atonement through an exposition of this epistle. In his 'subjective' theory Rom. 3.21 is taken to refer to God's love revealed in Christ. It evokes human faith and love, drawing believers into a loving relationship with God. Augustine too had understood Rom. 5.5 to refer to our love for God, rather than God's love for us. That is exegetically mistaken, but it is true to Paul's religion, summed up in the word 'grace', because that powerful word for attractiveness, goodness, favour, gift, goodwill, blessing, includes the loving response of gratitude. The Augustine who wrote 'Give me a man in love—he knows what I mean. Give me one who yearns; give me one who is hungry; give me one far away in this desert, who is thirsty and sighs for the Eternal country...'—he knew what Paul meant, and Abelard did too.

Paul's metaphors have been hardened into doctrine and his arguments applied to new situations, but the impact of Romans is not restricted to the history of doctrine. One purple passage or another in Paul has communicated Christianity more than many theological arguments.

That is not to underrate theology. Paul was a theologian and his successors have turned to him in developing their own theologies. But much of his theological language functions in new ways outside its original context and the heart of his religion will be found in his rhetoric. The theological arguments partly concealed in the 'right' language of Romans only became influential when with Augustine and Luther this was rediscovered as religion.

The more technical theological appeal to Romans is evident in the more analytic exegesis of the medieval scholastic theologians who worked through entire texts posing 'questions'. The scientific exactitude of St. Thomas' *Commentary on Paul* (still untranslated into English) is the high point, and feeds into his own theology. Rom. 1.19-20 provided support for his teaching that God's existence can be known to the light of reason, and Romans 4 with material for his salvation-history framework of belief.

St Thomas's opinion that God acts rationally, that is, in accordance with wisdom in saving humanity, was not the only view. Scotus and later Biel stressed the sovereignty of the divine will. Their combination of this voluntarism with an understanding of 'the justice of God' based on Cicero's definition of justice as 'rendering to each what is due' led to the interpretations of Romans which the young Luther inherited from his teachers in the so-called *via moderna*.

The explosive religious force of Luther's break with this scholastic theology around 1515 is first documented in his *Lectures on Romans* (1515–16, not published until 1908, English 1961). His new and distinctive understanding of justification is already emerging here in the claim that the Christian is at the same time righteous and a sinner, *simul iustus et peccator*, that is, extrinsically (in God's reckoning) justified, but intrinsically (as we are in ourselves and in our own estimation) sinners. That formulation is foreign to Paul and depends on reading Rom. 7 with the later Augustine as applying to Christian existence. Luther's insistence that justification is by faith *alone*, 'without the works of the law' (Rom. 3.28) is as old as Origen, but his understanding of faith and his polemical application of the doctrine against 'the law' are new and (in a way) true to Paul even though Luther meant more by 'the works of the law' than Paul probably intended.

Luther was much closer to Augustine than to Origen. His generalization of Paul's opposition to compulsory Torah observance for Gentiles, making 'works' apply to morality and catholic ritual and all human achievement, can be described as a radicalizing of Augustine's anti-Pelagian position. Its polemical edge was sharpened by an exegetically dubious blend of Romans with 1 Corinthians, but it remained within the possible parameters of medieval theological debate. It might have reformed the Western church without splitting it, but it coalesced with wider social and political factors, among them the birth of nation states, the new humanist learning, and the invention of printing which fed a new appetite for expositions of the newly available vernacular Scriptures.

Luther's later dispute with Erasmus over free-will (1525)—the radical Augustinian drawing on Rom. 9 to insist on predestination, against the sensible humanist who preferred the Greek Fathers—should not obscure the Reformers' great debt to the Renaissance. Melanchthon, Zwingli and Calvin were reforming humanists before they were protestant reformers. Everyone used the Greek text of Erasmus (1516) and was stimulated by his *Annotations*, or notes (e.g. on Rom. 5.12 and 9.5). Reform was in the air and scriptural interpretation at its heart.

Luther left his Catholic *Lectures on Romans* unprinted, and soon abandoned their Augustinian understanding of grace as healing, and their monastic emphasis on humility, based on the Psalter. It was his more widely expounded dialectic of law and gospel, and his correlation of the Word and faith, which placed Romans at the heart of Protestant theology, and made Paul on justification and faith the heart of the gospel for many Christians.

This Luther on Paul remains the fountain-head of Reformation exegesis and theology. He was closely followed by Tyndale. Melanchthon's *Loci Communes* of 1521, the first Protestant textbook of dogmatics, owed both its form and content to Romans as newly illuminated by Luther. Melanchthon's 1529 commentary reveals the friend of Erasmus in its use of classical rhetoric, whereas his *Apology* to the Augsburg Confession (1530) made his own forensic understanding of justification the standard Protestant view. It introduced the idea of 'imputation' on account of the alien merit of Christ (Article 21, para. 19). Instead of the catholic (Augustinian) 'making righteous' (by grace channelled through the sacraments) we have here the protestant 'pronouncing righteous' (Article 4, para. 252) mediated through the preached Word of God.

The centrality and disputed interpretation of this medieval doctrine of justification, and the importance of predestination for some of the Reformers, led to intensive exegesis of Romans from all sides. Like Melanchthon for Lutheranism, Calvin made Romans central for Reformed Christianity by his commentary (1540) and complementary *Institutes of the Christian Religion* (1536). The greatly enlarged edition of this systematic theology (1539) and its French translation (1541) included a chapter on justification by faith and one on predestination based on Romans and Augustine. Where Melanchthon was critical of the law Calvin defended it, and that inner-Protestant disagreement is reflected to this day in the commentaries of the Lutheran Käsemann and the Calvinist Cranfield.

After this short period of astonishing creativity the interpretation of Romans again reflected rather than propelled the history of doctrine. Justification remained the key doctrine for Lutherans, and Romans was read with reference to the individual, concentrating on chs. 1–8. As Luther had transferred Christian political responsibility to the state, Rom. 13.1-7 reinforced a conservative social and political stance. Elsewhere the Calvinist doctrine of predestination (cf. Rom. 8.28-29; 9.15, 18; 11.7) was challenged by Arminius

on a basis of his study of Romans; and it was also rejected by
Grotius, the Laudians and later Wesley. That deterministic
reading of Romans 9 had sustained both Reformers and puri-
tans under seige (as it had Augustine), but in England the
revolution was defeated and the more humane aspects of
Augustine prevailed in Anglicanism.

The religious potential of Paul's language was rediscovered
by both Lutherans and Reformed in pietism, and by the
Anglican John Wesley whose heart was 'strangely warmed'
in 1738 at the reading of Luther's Preface to Romans. All
these revivalists set such store by holiness or perfection as to
be accused by Calvinists of relapsing into 'works righteousness'. But their moral seriousness was true to Paul, even if
their separation of 'sanctification' (cf. Rom. 6.19, 22) from
justification, and seeing a structural division between
Romans 1–5 and 6–8 was mistaken. Wesley's recovery of
justification by faith for English Christianity was broadly
true to Romans as understood by Cranmer, whose homilies
he abridged and used as a summary of doctrine.

In Catholicism the Decree on justification at the Council of
Trent (1546–47) marked the end of compromise with
Protestantism and the end of convergence in their understanding of Romans. The Augustinian revival in Jansenism
brought some Catholic interpretation of Romans closer to
Protestantism, but its defeat contributed to the decline of
this Pauline language within Catholicism.

The doctrinal disagreements about justification were
echoed in commentaries on Romans into the present century.
Both the Catholic (made righteous, by grace) and the
Protestant (declared righteous by the judge) missed the
Hebrew background to Paul's Septuagint verb and the relationship character of his 'right' language. From the mid-
seventeenth century (Grotius in 1646, Hammond in 1653)
and especially with John Locke's glorious Preface (1705) to
the Epistles, some were learning to read Romans independently of their doctrinal commitments. Semler introduced
Morgan's theory (1737–40) about the difference between
Pauline and Petrine Christianity into Germany, and the
door was opened for the modern historical study of the
epistle, beginning with F.C. Baur's essay (untranslated)

on its 'purpose and occasion' (1836).

Baur's assessment of Romans was part of a grand theory about Christian origins best presented in his monograph on Paul (1845; English 1875). It had a huge influence on subsequent historical study but very little effect on the way Romans was read. Only lately have these same historical questions again been made decisive for understanding the epistle. Until recently Romans had continued to be read along traditional lines in conservative theology and preaching, and the decline of New Testament theology in late nineteenth-century liberal Protestantism meant a reduction in this epistle's influence in those circles. Interest in Paul's religion was still strong and the religious weight of Romans acknowledged, but the power of Augustine's and Luther's readings was lost when the theology of the epistle no longer much mattered. Wrede saw in 1904 that 'the religion of the apostle is theological through and through; his theology is his religion', but others were less discerning. They admired his genius but did not interpret his symbols.

In Barth's interpretation after the Great War (1919, 2nd edn 1921) the epistle regained the religious power and theological significance it had had for the Reformers and Wesley. A new era of New Testament theology began, centred on the Reformation interpretation of Romans. Its finest Pauline flowers were Bultmann's *New Testament Theology*, vol. 1 (1948; English 1952) and Käsemann's commentary (1973; English 1980).

By the 1970s a new mood briefly flickered in Western society, and so in its theology and biblical interpretation. Kerygmatic theology and hermeneutics seemed introverted, and 'changing society' the urgent task. This was nourished by biblical interpretation in Latin America, but in Western universities biblical scholarship invested more effort on its historical specialisms. A better understanding of Judaism has flourished, given a new impetus by the discovery in 1947 and gradual publication of the Dead Sea Scrolls. Monographs have multiplied as the profession of biblical studies has mushroomed. Few of them have seemed driven by the theological passion of a Luther, a Barth, or a Käsemann, but the new shape of Pauline studies has not been without theolog-

ical significance. Stendahl and Sanders have ensured
that appreciation of Paul's Jewishness (like Jesus') should
help transform the terrible record of Jewish–Christian
relations. Romans 11 has gained a central significance for
our generation, and has sometimes been misread to deny the
necessity of the Messiah Jesus for all.

The recognition that Second Temple Judaism was different
from, and more varied than what emerged as rabbinic
Judaism, has complicated attempts to do better justice to
Paul's Jewishness. And a better understanding of Paul's
socio-cultural and rhetorical contexts in the Greco-Roman
world are beginning to influence the exegesis and interpretation of Romans in new ways. Biblical scholarship today
displays a diversity of methods, outlooks and results as never
before, and this central New Testament text is second only to
Mark's Gospel in attracting the variety of approaches.

Scholarly study of the Bible, especially history and
exegesis, has driven theology along new paths, and this has
had some slight influence on religious practice and the wider
culture. But it is still Augustine's biblical theology, not
humanist scholarship, that has given Romans (especially
ch. 7) its influence on the history of philosophy (especially
philosophical anthropology), literature and psychology.
Discussions of 'fate, foreknowledge and free-will' have kept
Milton's devils and their successors occupied relating
Romans and human experience. And much of Augustine's
reading of Romans lurks in Kant, Dostoevsky, Kierkegaard,
Freud, and Heidegger. Religious art and music, by contrast,
have drawn almost nothing from this epistle.

The Christian churches, where Romans is read and valued
as Scripture, and even (in some quarters) as 'the clearest
gospel of all' (Luther), remain the locations where the impact
of the epistle is most persistent and direct, and also most
varied. The church's ongoing conversation with its Scripture
in the ministry of word and sacrament is shaped by the tradition of interpretation and by contemporary experience. The
ecological movement can find support from Romans 8, and
the movement for women's ministry encouragement from
Phoebe the deacon (16.1), but it is through its central
symbols that Romans continues to make its greatest impact.

Or through its tensions and antitheses. As we review the reception of Romans over nineteen centuries two theological giants stand out, in their similarities and differences. For all the continuities between Luther and Augustine, mediated through medieval theology, mysticism, monasticism and penitential practice, and later strengthened by the Reformer's study of his greater predecessor, the differences in their readings of Romans are important too. We may contrast the theologian of grace with the theologian of *faith alone*.

Luther's (and Paul's) *sola fide* presupposes a sola gratia and most emphatically a *solus Christus* but Luther's polemical antithesis between faith and works is sharper than Augustine's equally polemical use of the Pauline dialectic. Augustine stressed the positive side of Paul's antithesis, the gospel of grace and righteousness from God, the Spirit that gives life, the love of God that heals and transforms our will and gives us perfect freedom. The Pelagianism he confronted was not yet entrenched. When Luther wrote, Augustine's sense of the Pauline antithesis between law and grace (Rom. 6.14) had been partly lost in the medieval synthesis of nature and grace.

Christian theology almost always needs to be positive about law and has often read what Paul says about the law with spectacles borrowed from Aristotle. The positive statements about the law in Romans are helpful to a religion whose social functions include reinforcing restraint and motivating morality. But such a religion will always incline towards moralism in the perennial tension between giving moral guidance and celebrating the freedom which the Spirit brings (2 Cor. 3.17). It then needs to hear Paul's antithesis, whether accentuated positively as by Augustine, or justifiably sharpened as by Luther.

St Thomas, like most Christian theologians from St Luke and Irenaeus to the second Vatican council and beyond, have understood Paul's teaching within a framework of salvation-history. That is not wrong, since Paul shared that Judaeo-Christian framework, and often in Romans spoke of the law in those terms. But it tends to weaken the antithetical structure of Paul's central argument in Romans and especially in

Galatians, an argument which turns on a contrast between two kinds of religion or relationship with God: one which Sanders calls 'covenantal nomism', the other (more radically christocentric and charismatic) which Barth says 'has always stood on the brink of heresy' (p.13).

Nobody saw the antithetical structure of Paul's argument more clearly than Marcion. But he dissolved Paul's dialectic into a metaphysical dualism that cut the apostle (and also Jesus) loose from his Jewish context and presuppositions. Neither Luther nor the early Barth made that mistake, and yet both (as Barth confessed) had more than a whiff of Marcion about them. Paulinism, he observed, had always stood on the brink.

There are many worse places to stand. It is partly that which gives Romans and Galatians their cutting edge. Antithetical formulations in theology are always dangerous and usually one-sided; they are also sharp, and therefore useful in polemical situations. It is not by chance that Marcion, Augustine and Luther picked up Paul's antitheses in theological situations requiring (as they thought) *polemic*. How close they came to what was the heart of the matter for Paul himself is impossible to say. We do not know Paul in the way we know Augustine and Luther.

But in any case Paulin*ism* is not Paul. It consists in making the antithetical aspects of his thought the norm for understanding Christianity. The -*ism* is sufficiently perjorative to warrant reserving the word for those who add a *solus Paulus* to the other exclusive particle phrases. Marcion pleaded guilty and was locked out of the Catholic church. Luther and some of his followers seem on occasion to move in that direction. Any New Testament theology that makes Paul rather than the Gospels the centre of Scripture must seem suspect to mainline Christianity. Paul remains 'the apostle' par excellence, and the greatest theologian among the New Testament writers. But he remains one witness among many, and not even his greatest epistle has been as central as the gospels to the religious life of most Christians. His impact has been greatest in particular historical situations where his witness has seemed to some other genius most necessary, and most helpful for discrediting the theological opposition.

Our readings of this epistle have confirmed the validity of Augustine's and Luther's appeal to the dialectical structure of Paul's thought and the antithetical formulation of his argument, if not the generalizing character of their exegesis. It has also confirmed the validity of what gives their interpretations such religious power: the existential 'bite' of their concern with human experience. Paul is the only New Testament theologian to communicate the gospel in large part through anthropological terms. Sin and grace, faith and works, speak of human existence; letter and Spirit, law and gospel are closely aligned to that strong anthropological aspect to Paul's thinking.

At the same time, any interpretation which highlights Paul's understanding of human existence and salvation at the expense of his understanding of God and Christ is untrue to the apostle, however tempting to a secular culture and a 'religionless Christianity'. That misunderstanding is more likely to be evoked by the *sola fide* than by the *sola gratia* because faith is a human response, however experienced as a gift, whereas the gift or divine favour labelled grace is by definition inseparable from God the Giver.

Paul's understanding of God the Creator is not reducible to human self-understandings, and his knowledge of Christ is not reducible to a knowledge of his benefits. Humanity is not for Paul the measure of all things, and the freedom of which he, Augustine, Luther and the Book of Common Prayer ('whose service is perfect freedom') speak is far removed from the autonomy celebrated in the Enlightenment and some modern forms of Christianity. Paul's Christianity (our word, not his) is unashamedly religious and his religious symbols speak of God's gracious initiative before the human response of faith. God remains God and Paul can even use such unmodern metaphors as sovereignty and dominion. These are dangerous. They can lead to structures of domination. When this happens they too must be subjected to critical analysis and demolition by the children of God who are free.

If we are right to claim that the power of Paul's antithetical language has been most effective in polemical situations, such as those addressed by Marcion, Augustine, Luther and Barth, a final irony may be noted. For unlike Galatians, Romans itself is not a polemical writing. It is eirenic. We have argued that Paul is trying hard, without altering his fundamental conviction that salvation is *this* way (by faith in Christ), not *that* way (by Torah observance), to be conciliatory to the Jewish Christians in Rome (with an eye to Jerusalem).

The resolution of this paradox may be found in our claim that despite their considerable differences the best key to reading Romans is Galatians, where the polemical roots of Paul's antitheses are more clearly exposed. Marcion and Luther in effect read Romans through Galatians, and there is something profoundly right about that. The fundamental theological antithesis is the same in both epistles. On the other hand St Thomas and Calvin can appeal to the more conciliatory statements of Paul in Romans concerning the law. Augustine stands between them giving pointers in several directions. His emphasis on grace is true to Romans 5–7, and to Paul as a whole. Luther's emphasis on faith is true to Romans 1–11, but because it sharpens the negative ('not by works') it reflects the polemic of Galatians better than the conciliatory character of Romans. However, since both Paul in Romans and Augustine against the Pelagians stress both faith and the negative ('not by works') one can hardly criticize Luther for making that more explicit.

A historical explanation of why this polemical antithesis lies embedded in a conciliatory letter has been found in our account of its aims and historical context. That does not mean that Paul's theological antitheses were merely concerned with 'boundary markers' and 'entrance require-ments' for the Christian community, and that Paul is more interested in 'staying in' the new covenant community than in the character of the new relationship to God which this presupposes. 'Faith' for him described the whole of life in Christ, life in the Spirit, righteousness, sanctification or holy life, even if he derived his convictions about Christian exis-tence in part from the historical experience of Gentiles coming into the community and remaining Gentiles. Paul's powerful formulations have their roots in his experience and intentions. That is worth understanding, but should not licence a reductionism which explains away Paul's writing on the basis of its supposed motivations. He thought through his experience and missionary policy and worked them into a tolerably coherent theological statement. He supported them with what those who accepted his exegetical methods might accept as a cogent theological argument. This stands or falls by its internal consistency and its success or failure in persuading others.

It may not have been understood by or persuaded many, but it can now command respect from the historian of religion. His rhetoric proved more powerful, and that is partly how religion is communicated. What Paul had to say about the gospel can be epitomized in the powerful and positive word grace, as Augustine saw. And unlike glory, grace is built by Paul into his powerful antithesis. When that was relaxed in medieval theology it took a Luther to recover the polemical edge of the gospel with the truly Pauline phrase 'by faith alone'.

That could be the appropriate note on which to end, but a generation struggling to liberate itself from the Western religious tradition will not allow those formidable fathers the last word. Paul continues to be read by some who have consigned their interpretations of his symbols to the lumber room of Western religious history. What these scholars are beginning to see without doctrinal spectacles has a religious, moral and cultural value of its own.

Among many fresh insights emerging from modern historical study of Paul in his Jewish context is the recognition that neither individualism, nor guilt-ridden, soul-searching, morbid introspection, sexual hang-ups, metaphysical dualism, misogyny, nor anti-semitism, can be laid directly at the door of the historical Paul—though the ways in which he has been read have contributed to some of these. For example, while the frameworks of his thought are cosmic and community-oriented (as one would expect given his Jewish and Christian belief in God) his emphasis on faith in Christ as authentic response to God's saving intervention has a strongly individual thrust, and has contributed to Western religious individualism—which eventually became secularized. The autobiographical interpretation of Romans 7 is partly responsible (through Augustine) for 'the introspective conscience of the West', but since W.G. Kümmel's monograph on Romans 7 and Paul's conversion (1929; reprinted 1965) that view has increasingly been rejected. Paul valued sexual restraint more highly than many today, and he shared both the general Jewish rejection of homosexual practice and the patriarchal assumptions of his time and place (Jewish, Greek and Roman). He naturally regrets the majority of his nation's rejection of Christ, but pleads not guilty to the charge of disloyalty. Any suggestion of antisemitism is patently absurd, despite the bitter outburst of 1 Thess. 2.15-16 with its tragic echoes through subsequent history.

Paul's pessimistic assessment of the human situation outside Christ continues to cause offence. No doubt it is the reflex of his joyful message of salvation, but it is nonetheless real, and in the light of recent history many would add realistic. Sin has become a difficult term for a generation whose sense of God has been eroded, and some common religious metaphors for it, shared by Paul (such as defilement), seem strange. But religious systems are concerned with those aspects of human experience which this language symbolizes (failure and guilt) as well as with the finitude that leads many to yearn for resurrection. Even Marx could admit the human reality reference of religion as 'the sigh of the oppressed creature, the feeling of a heartless world, and the soul of soulless circumstances' (1844). Those who share Paul's symbolic realism and trust in the reality to which these religious symbols purport to refer will reject Marx's prejudice against transcendent reality but agree with his struggle against social injustice and his 'criticism of the valley of tears'. They may then be empowered through these symbols to work for a society that accords with them (cf. Rom. 12.2). Those for whom they are merely an opiate or an empty dream may, as the secular ideology is discredited, sadly miss the fundamental optimism that is sustained by Judaeo-Christian belief in God (cf. Rom. 8.31-39).

Rightly understood and lived this is not the easy optimism of a religious ideology, but a conviction learned in a tradition and tested and changed by experience. Paul speaks of a God who spared not his own Son (Rom. 8.32) and the evil powers which crucified him (1 Cor. 2.8). The reality of the cross is stamped upon the apostle's own body too (cf. Gal. 6.17). When Paul writes of 'affliction, hardship, persecution, hunger, nakedness, danger, or sword' (Rom. 8.35) it is six down and one to go for him personally (cf. 2 Cor. 11.23-27). The present evil age continues to exercise its power in a final assault that he understands as the birth-pains of the new age. He can even rejoice in his sufferings (5.2) with a hope that is not ashamed, and expects not to be disappointed. Those who want to understand inwardly the impact of Romans need only read again 5.1-11 and consider the comment of Paul's greatest interpreter: 'the apostle speaks with very great joy and gladness. In the entire Scripture there is hardly a text that equals this chapter, at least not in expression. For it describes most clearly the nature and extent of God's grace and mercy toward us' (*Lectures on Romans*, p. 153).

Recommendations for Further Reading

For a full, detailed historical orientation to Paul through his letters J. Becker, *Paul Apostle to the Gentiles* (1988, ET Louisville: Westminster/John Knox and London: SPCK, 1993), and J. Murphy O'Connor (Oxford: Oxford University Press, forthcoming) can be recommended. The best brief account is E.P. Sanders *Paul* (Oxford: Oxford University Press, 1991). More detail on Romans will be found in Sanders's brilliant monograph *Paul, the Law and the Jewish People* (Philadelphia: Fortress Press, 1983; London: SCM Press, 1985). A similar reorientation to Romans gained by considering Paul's attitude to the law is found in H. Räisänen, *Paul and the Law* (Tübingen: Mohr 1983, 1987; Philadelphia: Fortress Press) and F. Watson, *Paul, Judaism and the Gentiles* (Cambridge: Cambridge University Press, 1986). Behind them stands Sanders's great book on Judaism, *Paul and Palestinian Judaism* (London: SCM Press, 1977) and K. Stendahl, *Paul among Jews and Gentiles* (Philadelphia: Fortress Press, 1976; London: SCM Press, 1977) which includes his pioneering essay of 1963, 'The Apostle Paul and the Introspective Conscience of the West'. Among the Germans who resist it H. Hübner, *Law in Paul's Thought* (1978; English Edinburgh: T. & T. Clark, 1984) deserves mention.

Another admirable brief introduction is J. Ziesler's *Pauline Christianity* (Oxford: Oxford University Press, 1983, rev. edn 1990). This leads naturally into his simple and reliable commentary on Romans (London: SCM Press, 1989). Both take account of Sanders's pioneering work. C.K. Barrett's *Paul. An Introduction to his Thought* (London: Chapman, 1994) is far more weighty than its format suggests and sums up the best of traditional theological scholarship in a form appropriate to the study of Romans. Other excellent introductions include C. Roetzel, *The Letters of Paul* (Atlanta: John Knox, 1975, 1982; London: SCM Press, 1983) and L.E. Keck, Paul and his Letters (Philadelphia: Fortress Press, 1979, rev. edn 1988). Bible dictionaries are also helpful, and the articles on Romans by Roetzel in *Harper's Bible Dictionary* (1985) and by C.D. Myers in the *Anchor Bible Dictionary* (1992) are noteworthy. Also brief is L.T. Johnson *The Writings of the NT: An Interpretation*

(Philadelphia: Fortress Press; London: SCM Press, 1986), pp. 244-59 and 315-37.

Among recent commentaries in English, J.D.G. Dunn's large Word Commentary on the epistle (2 vols., 1988) with full bibliographies is responsive to the new climate. J.A. Fitzmyer's *Anchor Commentary* (1993) represents the best of American Roman Catholic scholarship and again contains weighty bibliographies. Among older commentaries available in English, C.E.B. Cranfield's ICC on the Greek text (2 vols.; Edinburgh: T. & T. Clark, 1975, 1979) contains most linguistic detail, and Käsemann's (1973; ET Grand Rapids: Eerdmans; London: SCM Press, 1980) the deepest theological penetration. There are many good shorter commentaries available, including those of C.H. Dodd (Moffatt, 1932), A. Nygren (1949), C.K. Barrett (Black, 1957), F-J. Leenhardt (1957), M. Black (1973), J.C. O'Neill (Penguin, 1975), J.A.T. Robinson (1979), R.A. Harrisville (Augsburg, 1980), P. Achtemeier (1985), P. Stuhlmacher (1989; ET 1994), J.R. Edwards (NIBC, 1992).

General works on Pauline theology focussed on Romans and pre-Barrett include J.C. Beker, *Paul the Apostle* (Philadelphia: Fortress Press; Edinburgh: T. & T. Clark, 1980). G. Bornkamm, Paul (1969; ET New York: Harper; London: Hodder, 1971), R. Jewett, *Paul's Anthropological Terms* (Leiden: Brill, 1971), and B. Witherington, *Paul's Narrative Thought World* (Louisville: Westminster/John Knox, 1994). All New Testament theologies contain plenty on Romans, especially those which treat Paul separately (e.g. Conzelmann, 1967, ET 1968; Kümmel 1969, ET 1974; Goppelt 1975–76, ET 1981–82; Stuhlmacher, vol. l, 1992; Hübner, vol. 2, 1993). Towering above them all, Bultmann's *Theology of the NT*, vol. 1 (1948, ET New York: Scribner; London: SCM Press, 1952) remains a classic, as does (from an earlier generation) A. Schweitzer, *The Mysticism of Paul the Apostle* (1930, ET 1931). Other relevant works of New Testament theology include C.F.D. Moule, *The Origin of Christology* (Cambridge: Cambridge University Press, 1977), G.D. Fee, *God's Empowering Presence* (Peabody, MA: Hendrickson, 1994) and K. Grayston, *Dying We Live* (London: Darton, Longman & Todd, 1990). For the social history W. Meeks, *The First Urban Christians* (New Haven: Yale University Press, 1983) is indispensable, and among hundreds of useful articles, those of N.A. Dahl, *Studies in Paul* (Minneapolis: Augsburg, 1977) and M.D. Hooker, *Studies on Paul* (Cambridge: Cambridge University Press, 1989) are excellent, and some of those in M.D. Hooker and S.G. Wilson (eds.), *Paul and Paulinism* (London: SPCK, 1982) pertinent.

On the literary genre of Romans see S.K. Stowers, *The Diatribe*

and Paul's Letter to the Romans (Chico, CA: Scholars Press 1981)
and W.G. Doty, *Letters in Primitive Christianity* (Philadelphia:
Fortress Press, 1973). Stowers's new book *A Rereading of Romans*
(New Haven: Yale University Press, 1994) will be discussed for
years. N. Elliott, *The Rhetoric of Romans* (Sheffield: JSOT Press,
1990) deserves similar close attention. Among the more experi-
mental writing on Romans G. Theissen, *Psychological Aspects of
Pauline Theology* (1983, ET Philadelphia: Fortress Press, 1987) and
H. Boers, *The Justification of the Gentiles* (Peabody,
MA: Hendrickson, 1994) are demanding.

In Chapter 3 of this Guide the material assembled by
K.P. Donfried (*The Romans Debate*, 1977, rev. edn Peabody, MA:
Hendrickson; Edinburgh: T. & T. Clark, 1991) was noted, as was
A.J. M. Wedderburn, *The Reasons for Romans* (Edinburgh: T. & T.
Clark, 1991). An older work of P.S. Minear, *The Obedience of Faith*
(London: SCM Press, 1971) may be added. On Chapter 4, R.B. Hays,
Echoes of Scripture in the Letters of Paul (New Haven: Yale
University Press, 1989) contains many insights. A full discussion of
it, with further bibliography, can be found in C.A. Evans and
J.A. Sanders (eds.), *Paul and the Scriptures of Israel* (Sheffield:
JSOT Press, 1993). More detailed analysis of Paul's citation tech-
nique is provided by C.D. Stanley, *Paul and the Language of
Scripture* (Cambridge: Cambridge University Press, 1992). The
older works of C.H. Dodd, *According to the Scriptures* (London:
Nisbet, 1952), B. Lindars, *New Testament Apologetic* (London: SCM
Press, 1961) and C.F.D. Moule, *The Birth of the New Testament*
(London: Black, 1962, rev. edn 1981), ch.4, are more readable.

On Paul's ethics or moral teaching V.P. Furnish, *Theology and
Ethics in Paul* (Nashville: Abingdon, 1968) and W. Schrage *The
Ethics of the NT* (1982, ET Philadelphia: Fortress Press; Edinburgh:
T. & T. Clark, 1988) are standard works indebted to Bultmann and
his pupils. J. Paul Sampley's recent paperback *Walking between the
Times: Paul's Moral Reasoning* (Minneapolis: Augsburg Fortress,
1991) is good and reliable. Wayne Meeks, *The Moral World of the
First Christians* (London: SPCK, 1987) provides essential back-
ground. Robin Scroggs, *The NT and Homosexualtiy* (Philadelphia:
Fortress Press, 1983) and V.P. Furnish, *The Moral Teaching of Paul*
(Nashville: Abingdon, 1979) tackle particular moral issues.

On the perspective suggested in Chapter 5, Gerd Theissen's essay
'Soteriological Symbolism in the Pauline Writings' (1977, ET in
Social Reality and the Early Christians [Minneapolis: Augsburg
Fortress, 1992; Edinburgh: T. & T. Clark, 1993]), C. Geertz,
'Religion as a Cultural System' (1966) reprinted in *The
Interpretation of Cultures* (New York: Basic Books, 1973) and else-

where, and L.T. Johnson, *Writings* may be singled out. Further details on some of the impact of Romans may be found in Alister McGrath's survey of the history of the doctrine of justification, *Iustitia Dei* (2 vols.; Cambridge: Cambridge University Press, 1986). An example of this impact or *Wirkungsgeschichte* may be read about in Harnack's *Marcion* (1921, ET 1989). But of the making of many books on Paul there is no end, and if all the books that betray his influence were listed there would probably not be a microchip in all the world to contain the books written.

So finally back to the text. Among the many modern translations rsv (or NRSV) and NEb (or REB) are authoritative but often disagree. Using both together is therefore instructive. Those interested in the textual criticism of Romans (Marcion ended with ch. 14, and the Chester Beatty Papyrus, P. 46, dated around 200, implies a tradition ending with ch. 15) should read Harry Gamble *The Textual History of the Letter to the Romans* (Grand Rapids: Eerdmans, 1977) and Bruce Metzger, *A Textual Commentary on the Greek New Testament* (United Bible Societies, 1971), pp. 505-41.

INDEXES

INDEX OF REFERENCES

OLD TESTAMENT

INDEX OF AUTHORS